THE WEARY ROAD

ALL RIGHTS RESERVED

THE WEARY ROAD

RECOLLECTIONS OF A SUBALTERN OF INFANTRY

By CHARLES DOUIE

INTRODUCTION BY
MAJOR-GENERAL SIR ERNEST SWINTON
K.B.E., C.B., D.S.O., R.E.

LONDON
JOHN MURRAY, ALBEMARLE STREET, W.

First Edition . . . 1929

AUTHOR'S PREFACE

AT the invitation of Mr. Carroll Romer, the Editor of the *Nineteenth Century and After*, I wrote early in 1928 an article on *The Soldier*. Another followed; eventually they numbered eight and appeared under the imposing title of *Memories of* 1914–1918. They were written in odd hours stolen from a life already too busy. I am much indebted to Mr. Romer not only for his encouragement, but for his indulgence when manuscript arrived late and afterthoughts found their way into proofs already overdue.

I have now endeavoured to make a book. To this end I have revised hasty judgments, effected some rearrangement, rewritten ill-considered passages, and added a substantial amount of new material. I hope that the book has been improved in these respects. I know that it has been improved, in a very marked degree, by the preface contributed by Major-General Sir Ernest Swinton, whose distinction as a soldier and a writer is known to all, and by the reproduction on the wrapper of Sir William Orpen's great drawing *Man Thinking on the Butte-de-Warlencourt*, by his permission and that of the Director of the Imperial War Museum.

The record here set down covers the period of the war, but the major part of it is concerned with quite a short period. The reason is partly that my pious intention of keeping full notes went the way of most pious intentions at an early date, and partly that first impressions have the most lasting effect on the mind. There was no billet quite like the first billet, no sector of trenches to compare with the first sector in interest and excitement, no bombardment so majestic and impressive as the first bombardment. Custom had power to stale and to render tedious experiences which had at first almost a romantic interest, and the routine of war as little merits vain repetition as the routine of peace.

C. O. G. D.

ZERMATT
21st August 1929

CONTENTS

	PAGE
Author's Preface	v
Introduction by Major-General Sir Ernest Swinton	ix

CHAPTER I
The Soldier 1

CHAPTER II
The First Year 24

CHAPTER III
Early Days 44

CHAPTER IV
The Dorset Regiment . . . 68

CHAPTER V
Winter on the Somme . . . 86

CHAPTER VI
A City of the Dead . . . 109

CHAPTER VII
SPRING IN PICARDY 130

CHAPTER VIII
FIGHTING ON THE ANCRE . . . 154

CHAPTER IX
THE MARSHES OF THE YSER . . 177

CHAPTER X
DAWN ON ASIAGO 202

INTRODUCTION

By Major-General Sir Ernest Swinton K.B.E., C.B., D.S.O.

Some months ago I chanced to pick up a copy of *The Nineteenth Century and After* containing the last instalment of a series of articles entitled " Memories of 1914–1918," by C. O. G. Douie. Most of us who are old enough have our own memories of that period, and have read a certain number of the reminiscences recorded by others ; and it was without any very keen anticipation that I started to peruse what had been set down by Mr. Douie. By the time I had finished I was so impressed that I obtained the preceding instalments in order to prolong the enjoyment and feeling of satisfaction given to me by what I had read.

The publication of this series of articles in book form under the title of *The Weary Road* is in my opinion an event in the course of the comparatively thin stream of war literature produced in the English language—thin because the output has not, either in quantity or in quality, corresponded to the nature of the subject. It is a matter for congratulation on account of the intrinsic value and interest of what the author has to say. Moreover, the moment of the appearance of the book is opportune.

Mr. Douie, as a young and impressionable man, served through the war, on the Western Front—where warfare was waged in its most intense form,—and in Italy. He was in the fighting line, and rose to the command of a company in that Arm, the infantry, which has in the past usually borne the brunt of the battle and in the Great War most certainly did. He is, therefore, by personal experience and first-hand knowledge well equipped to speak. So far as other qualifications are concerned, the style and the tone of his writing, the breadth and depth of his point of view, show him to be an observer with a balanced, reflective mind and one gifted with great powers of analysis. His descriptions, without being overloaded with " purple," are realistic and graphic, and will bring back poignantly to many of his readers the events and scenes of past years. And he has further qualifications which specially commend what he has to tell us.

Speaking of the armies of 1914,—of which he is a doughty champion, though not an old Regular himself, he says :

INTRODUCTION

> "Those Armies are silent; death has taken toll of all but a remnant, and that remnant, never very articulate, have now no spokesman who has the literary gifts to tell their story with justice and truth."

That, unfortunately, seems to be correct. So far as the New Armies are concerned, however, we have in Mr. Douie one who does possess those literary gifts in a marked degree. But more even than in the ability to write he is blessed with insight and sympathy. He knows the temperament and mentality of the soldiers —the average British men, of whom he was one, and for whom he speaks; and can project himself into their minds. He reveals to us their reactions to the war as a whole and to the immediate dreadful circumstances in which they found themselves. He voices the feelings and sentiments which the great majority have neither the ability nor the desire to impart to others. He gives to us the point of view of the hundreds of thousands of men who were in the thick of things, and acted and suffered as they did at the prompting of and in the exaltation of their own souls, or in confidence at the bidding of those higher up. He does not take us behind the scenes or make revelations as to the higher leading or the conduct of operations. Many other books have done that,

And he does not unnecessarily accentuate all that is foul and bestial in war. His work, beyond being a graphic narration of events, is an instructive commentary, devoid of undue bitterness and a sane presentment of the psychology of the British fighting man.

This volume appears opportunely because it serves as a timely corrective to the possible influence of one or two widely read German war books which have recently been translated. One writer—a brilliant artist—by concentrating on the material side of war and an overemphasis on all that is squalid, unpleasant or merely unimportant in life—has succeeded in giving us a one-sided picture, quite ignoring the " something higher " which enabled human beings to withstand the horrors so meticulously detailed. Another, by his hectic, disconnected, staccato style, gives the impression of having written under the influence of hysteria. That such works are probably not typical of the German war-complex generally is shown by yet another book *The Storm of Steel* by Captain Ernst Jünger. This, in its glorification of the war spirit, perhaps goes to the other extreme ; but it does make clear what inspired and enabled human beings to carry on at all and to sacrifice themselves for a cause.

But whether these books convey an entirely fair idea of the German character or not, they are sufficient to give us some conception of it, and *The Weary Road* comes to us at the right moment to show how very different it is from ours, and to confirm in unmistakable terms the striking contrast. It is a relief to have the staid, solid British point of view, which lies between the two extremes of despairing disillusionment and perfervid exaltation. It is therefore doubly welcome.

Deeply as he interests us, Mr. Douie does more. In amplifying and illustrating what he wishes to express by numerous quotations from some of the finest things already written on the subject in the English language, he leads us on and upwards. His book, written from the heart, with deep conviction, is cheering. It is essentially an act of justice and a tribute to our million dead. It tells us something of what they cannot tell us, of what the vast inarticulate majority of those who still live cannot tell us. It tells us in what manner and why they rose above pain and fear and gave themselves—mostly unconscious of their own high motives.

To those of its readers who have sad cause to look back it will bring comfort and not despair. From all it deserves gratitude.

E. D. S.

CHAPTER I

THE SOLDIER

On the occasion of the dedication of the new Menin Gate at Ypres Lord Plumer delivered a brief but memorable address. No man more suited to the task could have been chosen. During the greater part of the war he had commanded the forces defending the salient; and the one mitigating feature of service in that dismal and dangerous sector of the Western Front was the personality of the army commander. There were but few of the Second Army present at the Menin Gate, but there were 400,000 not far away. And of these, and of every soldier who never returned from our far-flung battle line, Lord Plumer said: " He is not missing. He is here."

To the soldier these words meant much. The circumstances of his life, and the traditions of his service, render him distrustful of oratory. He has forgotten, if indeed he ever heard or read, the speeches of his political leaders, which will be of such interest and importance to the historian. If asked during the war why he had joined the Army, he was accustomed to make a facetious response, knowing well that the kind of person whose regard he valued would not believe him. The impression likely to be left on the minds of other persons (whose regard he did not value) was a matter of no consequence to him. Unfortunately, these other persons for a variety of reasons have received much attention since the war, and there is a common impression that the soldier had no idea of the issues at stake and joined the Army in a moment of over-excitement, only to repent for ever afterwards. The truth is that the soldier was so conscious of the issues at stake, and felt so strongly on the subject, that he was at pains to conceal his real feelings.

To the New Armies of 1914 it was enough that their country was at war, and that something which they valued far more than life was in jeopardy. The spirit of England in those tragic days was expressed very adequately in John Masefield's great poem, August 1914. The "English city never built by hands," though but dimly understood, was to the soldier a thing at once too precious to discuss and well worthy of that sacrifice which he was called upon to make on its behalf. Through four years of hardship and danger he was supported in his faith, not by the stimulus of oratory, but by his sense of comradeship with those who were with him steadfast in that faith. To them only did he listen, and their words remain in his mind. Chief among them perhaps were those memorable words in which the Commander-in-Chief of the British Forces in France addressed his battle-worn troops in the darkest hour of the war:

"There is no other course open to us but to fight it out. Every position must be held to the last man: there must be no retirement. With our backs to the wall and believing in the justice of our cause, each one of us must fight on to the end. The safety of our homes and the freedom of mankind alike depend upon the conduct of each one of us at this critical moment."

To those words the soldier responded in full confidence in his Chief. Ten years later the soldier will believe the best loved of his fellow soldiers, though the evidence of the truth of his words is far to seek.

"He is not missing. He is here." Surely Lord Plumer meant that the spirit of the soldier is ever present in our midst, that his courage and devotion, his Stoic creed of silence and fortitude, inspire the daily life of our generation, have become the heritage of generations yet unborn. The literature of the day gives no support to the idea; can the soldier be right and the trained observer be wrong? The war is regarded as an improper subject for conversation; and all references to it are discouraged except on Armistice Day. On one day of the year the dead at least have their meed of honour; the living are without honour even on that day.

In our schools every boy and girl learns something of an heroic past. Salamis and Marathon and Thermopylæ are familiar names to boys who have never heard, and never will hear, of the grim and steady ranks who kept the Germans from the sea in the First Battle of Ypres and again in the long agony of the fighting on the Somme and the Lys in the spring of 1918. Were the Spartans at Thermopylæ more resolute than the Worcesters at Gheluvelt, than the 4th Guards Brigade, surrounded, fighting back to back against hopeless odds, but gaining the few hours which enabled the Australians to detrain and the advance on Hazebrouck to be stayed? Why should the name of Leonidas be honoured more than the name of the Colonel under whose leadership the 2nd Devons, 28 officers and 525 men, fought to the last on the Aisne in May of 1918 in " unhesitating obedience to orders," to win from the French General Berthelot a tribute well worthy of record in our literature and from the French nation the unprecedented honour of the Croix-de-Guerre? And these are but three out of many records of which every soldier could tell. The story of the blocking of Zeebrugge on St. George's Day, 1918, is unknown to boys who know every incident in the destruction of the Great Armada. Is an heroic present so much less worthy of study than an heroic past?

The major issue of the war, so far as our country was concerned, was the menace to our national life denoted by the control of the Low Countries by the strongest Power in Europe. Every schoolboy knows that the wars of Marlborough were fought over that issue; why should he not be told that that was the political issue of fifteen years ago? The answer commonly given to these questions is, " At all costs we must discourage militarism. Let the great ideals of the League of Nations be set before the young. References to the justice of our cause, and to the courage and devotion of those who fought, cannot but encourage a martial spirit and make another war inevitable." To this the soldier may well reply that he attaches more importance to the outlawing of war than any other body of men. He has seen all that war can show in the way of horror, pain, and death. But day by day, in the dire extremity which was his lot, he learned the importance of truth. In a sheltered life a man may base his life upon a lie for years and suffer no harm. In the hour of battle a man has need of the truth. If we tell lies about the war to our children, we will be found out some day. Peace cannot be built upon the shifting sands of misrepresentation. Even if it were true that the war was a discreditable episode in our history, and that the soldier was an unfortunate and much-deceived person, would this discourage a martial spirit in the younger generation? It is much more likely to have precisely the opposite effect, for the younger generation may feel it incumbent on them to retrieve our forfeited pride as a nation. Let the rights and wrongs of our policy for fifty years before the war be discussed with every frankness. Let the merits and prospects of the League of Nations be discussed with an equal candour. But let the younger generation know that there never was a body of men less imbued with militarism than the Armies of 1914, and that they fought, suffered, and died in the belief that they were defending not only the right of their country to order its own affairs, but the hard-won emancipation of the free peoples of the world from militarism. Whether they were right or wrong in their judgment may be discussed to the end of time; the spirit in which they went to war is hardly a matter of doubt.

But here literature takes up the tale. Book after book is published in which that spirit is denied. In poetry and prose alike the real life of the soldier has been " revealed " by men who have honestly thought that they were doing a service to their late comrades, and to humanity, by describing in intimate detail scenes of carnage and degradation, by dwelling on all that was most horrible in war. It is well that such books should be written. They redress the balance of the old literature of war. They atone for the wrong done by all of us to those at home, when we wrote letters in which war was depicted as a series of hilarious incidents, and the bloodshed, danger, and physical infamies of battle and of life in a trench line were never mentioned. They destroy the legend, created under pressure by the war-correspondents, of the gallant, laughing troops eager to be at the enemy again, almost mutinous because another battalion has been given the most dangerous sector of the battle line. But the authors of this poetry and prose of horror and carnage have overstated the case in quite as great a degree as we understated it during the war. The sight of blood has gone to their heads. They can see nothing else. But a man may shed worse things than blood. The sight of a man who has lost his self-respect is far more repugnant than the sight of a brave man, dirty and bleeding. Peace offers many opportunities of seeing the former, more opportunities in my experience than war. Peace has also its horrors, greater than the horrors of war, as any doctor or nurse can tell. War gave us in full measure much that we would wish to forget in the way of sorrow and suffering. But war gave us also in recompense and in as full a measure memories of courage and high fellowship. War conferred on us also the opportunity of honourable and disinterested service, of duty faithfully discharged, which carried with it the great gift of the tranquil mind. I know that many, I believe that most, soldiers would say at the end of the weary road which for four years they trod, what a certain Pilgrim said after passing through the Slough of Despond and the Valley of the Shadow of Death, "Yet now I do not repent me."

There have been books on the war which hold the balance, which show both sides of the soldier's life. *The First Hundred Thousand, Undertones of War, The Adventures of an Ensign, The Way of Revelation,* are examples. The two latter books, written by officers in the Guards, are admirable correctives to the literature which speaks only of the degradation and disillusion of war. They show war in all its horror and carnage, but they reveal also the dominance of the spirit of man over things material, the resolution which met and mastered demands unparalleled before, the courage which triumphed over pain and death. They pay just tribute to the memory of the 7,000 tall guardsmen whose names are written on the memorial at Lesbœufs which records the dead of the Battles of the Somme.

There is a poetry of the war which within its limited range attains real greatness. But the poetry is for the most part forgotten and books on the war are supposed to have no chance with the reading public. Indeed the literature of the last eight years virtually ignores the existence of any war background to the lives of this generation. The defence of the city-state of Athens against the Persians was coincident with the flowering of the Attic genius in Æschylus and Sophocles. The England of the Tudors, victorious on the seas and for the first time heralding her destiny as a nation, gave us Shakespeare. At the time of a nation's greatest vitality literature has hitherto had no unworthy share. Was not Æschylus a better poet because he had served in the ranks at Marathon? Were not the dying words of Sir Philip Sidney at the battle of Zutphen the words of a poet? In this age England has at least shown a great vitality. The gathering of a free people from five continents is evidence which no man can gainsay. Are the prose and poetry of this age to be charged with disillusion and despair?

The reason is not far to seek. The hand of death has been heavy on those who had the greatest literary gifts. The prayer of R. E. Vernède was the prayer of the war poets:

> All that a man might ask thou hast given me, England,
> Yet grant thou one thing more;
> That now when envious foes would spoil thy splendour,
> Unversed in arms, a dreamer such as I
> May in thy ranks be deemed not all unworthy,
> England, for thee to die.

For the most part they obtained that which they sought. The war was not nine months old when Julian Grenfell and Rupert Brooke passed into the Silence. The greatness of the loss to our literature we can hardly tell. Surely no anthology of English poetry can omit *The Soldier*:

> If I should die, think only this of me,
> That there's some corner of a foreign field
> That is for ever England. There shall be
> In that rich earth a richer dust concealed;
> A dust whom England bore, shaped, made aware,
> Gave, once her flowers to love, her ways to roam,
> A body of England's, breathing English air,
> Washed by the rivers, blest by suns of home.

Yet more splendid perhaps is *Into Battle*, with its prophetic close:

> The thundering line of battle stands
> And in the air death moans and sings,
> But Day shall clasp him with strong hands
> And Night shall fold him in soft wings.

THE SOLDIER

A few days after writing this great poem Julian Grenfell, as great a soldier as he was a poet, the lineal successor of Sir Philip Sidney, lay dying of wounds, and the watchers by his bedside heard dimly on his lips the lines from the Hippolytus :

> Oh ! for a deep and dewy spring,
> With runlets cold to draw and drink,
> And a deep meadow blossoming
> Long-grassed, and poplars in a ring
> To rest me by the brink.

For a brief hour the soldier and the poet were one after three hundred years.

The loss of Julian Grenfell and Rupert Brooke was irreparable, but the tale of our losses was not complete. Charles Sorley fell at Loos, W. N. Hodgson on the first day of the Somme, and Allen Seager met his long-sought " rendezvous with death " almost in the same hour. They were followed by E. W. Tennant, R. E. Vernède, and many another through whose literary talents some record might have been left of the faith and fire of the Armies of 1914. Those armies are silent ; death has taken toll of all but a remnant, and that remnant, never very articulate, have now no spokesman who has the literary gifts to tell their story with justice and truth.

Great writers of established reputation have attempted to put the point of view of the soldier, either in war or on his return to a settled life, but it is no discredit to them as artists that they have failed really to understand him, or to appreciate that his attitude of mind derives from experience which they have not shared. For many of us the most important, the formative years of our life were spent under conditions similar to those of primitive man, living in holes in the ground, exposed to sun, wind, and rain, surrounded by watchful enemies, for ever in the presence of disaster and death. We learned to hold in high honour some virtues no longer of much account in a protected community—courage, fidelity, loyalty to friends. Death was to us a byword. Our lives were forfeit, and we knew it. Life has never presented itself in this guise to men living in urban communities. The very atmosphere of a battlefield defies description and eludes the imagination. It is easy to talk of the thunder of the barrage, of the staccato rhythm of the machine guns, of the crash of exploding bombs, of the cries of the wounded, of the blended majesty and horror which inform a modern battlefield. But words cannot convey even a suggestion of the sounds heard and of the emotions felt, when every faculty is heightened, when every nerve is tense. The hour of battle cannot be described; it is an experience open only to those who meet it.

Rudyard Kipling is a great artist, whose imagination has taken him into the minds of many wayward people, whose powers of description have created for his readers the very atmosphere of strange places and unfamiliar scenes. Of the great writers who have made the soldier of the recent war the theme of a book, he has come nearest to an appreciation of war from a soldier's point of view. In his book *The Irish Guards in the Great War* the morale of the Guards is splendidly depicted. But his description of the battle of the Somme and of the part played by the Irish Guards at Ginchy and Lesbœufs in September 1916 is not to be compared with the superb narrative to be found in *The Adventures of an Ensign* by the anonymous "Vedette." Yet the insight of Rudyard Kipling has shown him, as it has not shown other writers of established reputation, that the soldier has a distinct point of view, based on experiences other than their own, that he lives in a world apart, a world denied to the older generation and to the younger. In the last words of his book, describing the march past of the Guards Division in London in the summer of 1919, he speaks of men in civilian clothes standing in the crowd—" Young men with eyes that did not match their years, shaken beyond speech or tears by the splendour and the grief of that memory."

When many of our greatest writers have failed to see those young men, is it small wonder that they pass unnoticed in a busy world? Yet they are there for those who wish to see. On Armistice Day they are numerous, though as ever inarticulate. I have seen many of them at the war films—quiet, not applauding, hoping, so far as I could judge, not to be noticed. Instinctively the soldier recognises other soldiers; the dignity of their one-time calling has given to them a carriage of the head which cannot be mistaken; their tragic experience has written in their eyes a certain weariness, yet those eyes are clear and free from illusion; their manner is quiet, as is fitting to men conscious of their proven manhood; there is an air of high memory about them, the remnant of a great fellowship, the custodians of a proud tradition. The soldier will talk of his war experiences to other soldiers; indeed, when he meets them he talks of little else; to those who did not share those experiences he will say nothing, because he is anxious not to suggest in any way that he is a person deserving of special consideration, that there is any occasion for gratitude. Indeed, he would deny that there is a debt; he would say that his own generation stood to lose most if freedom had fallen, if England had not lived. But this unwillingness to remind a happier generation of the price which was paid for their happiness has perhaps made the soldier unmindful of his duty to keep alive the memory of his friends. It is a debt which he owes to them.

> If thou didst ever hold me in thy heart,
> Absent thee from felicity awhile,
> And in this harsh world draw thy breath in pain
> To tell my story.

Contemporary writers have failed to grasp that the soldier has these memories ; they have gone farther, they have attributed to him a disillusion which they feel have called upon him to voice their own bitterness. When the soldier came back from the war he was very tired. Victory had come late—not too late, but still long deferred. The morale of the Army, as a whole, remained magnificent throughout the last year of the war. In all armies some regiments are better than others, and there may have been unreliable infantry battalions, though, if there were, they were few and far between. No one will say that the Army of 1918 was the equal in fighting quality of the Army of 1916. Still it was good enough to sustain a defensive battle against a great superiority of numbers on the Somme and the Lys, and to return to the attack and remain continuously on the offensive from August to November. The infantry at least had no doubt that they were winning, and their faith was justified when the greatest military Power of modern times collapsed finally in disordered retreat after the battles of the Sambre and the Selle. It is clear from books which have been written since that the morale of the infantry did not communicate itself to all those who enjoyed at once a greater security and a wider view of the situation. But the morale of the infantry was bought at a great price ; keyed up to endeavour far beyond their normal powers, marching and fighting over great tracts of country throughout the last year, they suffered the inevitable reaction when their task was done and they might rest. Those of us who spent the first Armistice Day on the battlefield have in our minds scenes very different from those common in London, Paris, and other great cities. Most soldiers will speak of the unwonted silence, for the first time unbroken by gun or rifle fire after four long years. The civil population remembers Armistice Day for the most part in terms of noise.

But the soldier was too tired to be elated ; he was none the less deeply conscious of victory and of the freeing of the world from that menace which he had fought for so long, to defy which so many of his friends had died. On his return home he was still very weary, and those who had little knowledge of the soldier's life, and less insight into his mind, observing his weariness, mistook it for disillusion. The literature of the day may be charged with disillusion, but the soldier must disclaim responsibility for it. He has said little or nothing; he has gone on his way, sharing his memories with other soldiers, content that he did not fail in the great task to which he set his hand, that he was not false to that great fellowship which he was once privileged to share.

Some writers are prepared to admit that the soldier did not find victory the great illusion, but fall back on a second line, asserting that the soldier has learned disillusion since, principally in the Treaty of Versailles, but also in the widespread unemployment of so many of his comrades.

In one of these issues the soldier has, I am afraid, taken less interest than he might have been expected to take. The Treaty of Versailles may have been iniquitous; Sir Ian Hamilton in his eloquent denunciation of it may have expressed the feelings of the soldier, or rather the feelings which would have been those of the soldier if he had read it. But the soldier took little interest in the peace; he had entered on a war to combat a menace. The menace was removed, he was content that the politicians should undertake a task for which they had a penchant, if not a capacity. Nor had he those high hopes of a world made safe for democracy, particularly German democracy, which earnest-minded people have attributed to him. He was prepared to fight, and to sacrifice his life, for the security of his country and the destruction of the militarism which happened to threaten it. But his interest in democracy has been exaggerated. He would have been shocked had he realised that his late enemies were being " kicked when they were down," but, as the British Army was not engaged in that pursuit on the Rhine, it did not occur to him that the process was being pursued in the interminable clauses of a treaty.

Unemployment is another matter. Here the soldier has real excuse for bitterness. He realises that the soldier must take his share of the unemployment brought about by hard times, but he has reason to believe, and good reason, that he has been called upon to shoulder a disproportionate share of the burdens of peace. The brunt has fallen, moreover, as it fell in the war, on the infantry. The man who made munitions, and the man with a trade, who found his way during the war for the most part into the Royal Engineers, Royal Army Service Corps, and other technical services, has been absorbed without difficulty into industry. The infantry were drawn largely from the ranks of the general labourer, and they included a vast body of men who might have entered a skilled trade, but forfeited their chance by joining the Army as soon as they became of military age. It is an unhappy thought that many of the men who never lost heart in the darkest hours of 1918, fighting their country's enemies, have been brought almost to despair in the face of another enemy, an enemy which must be fought without the support either of the old comradeship or the old faith. England may well bow her head in shame at the thought of her 21,000 disabled unemployed.

It is true that disillusion has been brought about to a limited extent by that forgetfulness and neglect. But the soldier knows that much has been done, and the great majority of his comrades have found employment, and even among those who have not there is an amazing absence of genuine bitterness. Indeed, a clear view of the war, unobscured by bitterness, is quite common among soldiers, and if at any time in the future literature is to enable posterity to see the war steadily and to see it whole, the soldier is more likely to provide the material than the non-combatant. The Armies of 1914 were on the whole free from bitterness. Of chivalry, in the sense understood by romantic mediævalists, there was none, except perhaps in the clean warfare of the air. But there was respect for an enemy whose bravery, tenacity, and devotion to his country were not in doubt.

Among the fighting men bitterness was least; it increased steadily through the various degrees of security until genuine ferocity was achieved by non-combatants who had neither part nor lot in the war. Men whose business it was to take another man's life were not interested in taking away also his character. Men and women who had sent their sons to the war, and lived in ever-present anxiety, often to be resolved only by a life-long sorrow, did not forget that there were men and women among their country's enemies whose daily lot did not differ from theirs. Bitterness is more often caused by frustration than by suffering. Those to whom the tragedy of the war was most keen reached heights of suffering and sorrow which were far beyond the range of bitterness.

The soldier has other memories of which he prefers to say nothing. He may deny that there is a debt owing to him from his country; but he is deeply conscious that he owes a debt, and one which cannot ever be fully paid, to the dead. He knows well that in the main they were the best, the natural leaders. The cliffs of Gallipoli, the slagheaps of Loos, the chalk uplands of the Somme, hold for ever the citizen armies of August and September 1914—the men to whom the dreadful necessities of the hour were most immediately clear, the advance guard of a nation in arms. In those armies were the men of whom we stand in such crying need to-day—the fearless, the disinterested, the eager. The leadership which the possession of those qualities naturally conferred upon them brought with it almost certain death. How well we remember those men, who would not be denied, the first to volunteer for a hazardous enterprise, the last to leave the untenable position! Wounded time and again, they returned to the front; disabled for infantry fighting, they took up flying; reduced to a sedentary life, they insisted on following it in kite balloons. In March 1918 the corridors of the War Office were filled with discharged and disabled men, demanding to be sent back to their old regiments. Is it small wonder that these, the natural aristocracy of their generation, are but a memory? We who are left know well that we would not be here if we had been as good men as they, and we falter on a path which under their leadership we had once the courage to follow. Remembering them, we may recapture a little of the morale of this island race at the moment of its greatest peril and highest achievement:

> Thank Him, who isled us here and roughly set
> His Briton in blown seas and storming showers;
> We have a voice with which to pay the debt
> Of boundless love and reverence and regret
> To those great men who fought and kept it ours.

We have a voice, we who are left, for we have but to name our friends, and the memories which their names evoke are more eloquent than poetry. But there is no voice which can tell our story to those who come after us; the men who might have had that power are dead, their voices are stilled for ever. Lord Plumer is right. " He is not missing. He is here." But he is here only so long as his memory rests in the minds of those who were intimate with him whether in the home or on the battlefield. When the generation who fought the war is dead much will perish which might be of value to those who come after us. Is no record to be left ?

Records there are in thousands in the form of letters and diaries. No one will ask that the letters may be published; they were intended usually for one person alone. The diaries are for the most part unsuited to publication; they lack literary form. Yet, rough as they are, they may be of interest, and at some future date may be of service if a writer of genius should attempt to set on the stage the lofty scene of the Great War, as in *The Dynasts* Thomas Hardy has set the Napoleonic Wars for our contemporaries.

In this conviction I have set down in these pages a record of undistinguished service in Belgium, France, and Italy of a soldier whose highest command was that of a company of infantry. My hope is that its publication may induce other soldiers of wider experience and greater literary merit to put on record their memories of the war. The record of our tragic experience may help our children : we could not save ourselves ; we may yet save them. The beacons of peace are aflame for the younger generation ; if they turn to the pages of *The Shropshire Lad* they may learn by whose hands the beacons were lit.

> Now, when the flame they watch not towers
> About the soil they trod,
> Lads, we'll remember friends of ours
> Who shared the work with God.
>
> To skies that knit their heartstrings right,
> To fields that bred them brave,
> The saviours come not home to-night :
> Themselves they could not save.

CHAPTER II

THE FIRST YEAR

MEMORY is reported to play havoc with human experience : it is merciful in that it rejects so much that was painful ; it is kindly in that it retains so much that conferred pleasure ; it is humorous in that it gives importance to our small share in events at which we were present, and secures our attendance at events which we unhappily missed. George IV derived much satisfaction from his reminiscences of the Battle of Waterloo ; and many of us in the course of years will become convinced that we were first under fire on August 23, 1914, on the Mons-Condé Canal, and that we took part in all the subsequent engagements of the next four years, ultimately entering Mons again on the morning of Armistice Day.

The casualty lists will be there to deny our stories ; at one time the average life of the infantry subaltern in a division in the line on the Somme was reported to be less than three weeks. But if our memories play us these tricks, we have this excuse, that the infantry soldier saw less of the strategy of the war, and indeed of the progress of a battle, than any man in England who had a penny to spare for an evening paper. For a mile on each side of him he saw everything; beyond that nothing. If the battle went well in his immediate neighbourhood, he was convinced of victory; if it went ill, of defeat. If hopes were often dupes, fears were more often liars.

Moreover, the limited view which the circumstances of the infantry soldier's life imposed on him has a further effect on the historical value of his recollections. He was rendered incapable of seeing the course of events in a true perspective and of distinguishing between events of great and small consequence. A staff officer could envisage a battle in progress with a front of perhaps thirty miles and with far-reaching results, tactical and strategic. The infantry soldier, in his own phrase, "went over the top." The consequences to himself, his company, and his battalion were not greatly different whether the engagement was of small or of great importance. My regiment was most heavily engaged and suffered severe losses on several days of the war which are not accounted historic. The interest of the infantry soldier is naturally in those engagements rather than in battles which had a decisive effect on the progress of the war, but in which his regiment was not called upon to play a prominent part. Moreover, losses were often severe on occasions which are not dignified by the title of battle on the colours of a regiment. A period of trench warfare in certain sectors, such as Hooge, St. Eloi, the Hohenzollern Redoubt, and La Boisselle, might be more costly and far more trying than a major engagement.

The first five battle-honours of the 1st Dorset Regiment in the war are Mons, Le Cateau, Retreat from Mons, Marne, Aisne. The total casualties (including missing) in these battles were 261. We lost approximately the same number of killed and wounded in a short period of trench warfare (less than two months) at Ypres. " Hill 60 " and Damery are not named in the roll of battles of the war. Yet the fighting at Hill 60 in May and June 1915 cost the regiment 25 officers and 558 men, of whom 148 were killed or died of wounds on the occasion of the successful defence of May 1. In August 1918 in the assault on Damery the regiment lost 8 officers and 26 men killed and 289 wounded and missing. Yet the name of the village has no significance except to those who were there.

Memories of the war, so far as the infantry soldier is concerned, cannot be set out in terms of battles. The events which have left most impression on his mind are often quite trivial.

Their significance is largely personal to himself and difficult to explain. The memories of the war which I have here set down are not intended to support any strategical theory of the conduct of the war ; they throw no new light on the fortunes of any battle ; they are of no value to the military historian.

The tricks of memory and the limited field of vision of the infantry soldier are not the only circumstances which compel me to seek the indulgence of the reader. My mind was far from mature when it received the impressions here set down. The war effectually put an end to my education. If I have a philosophy of life, it is based, not on wide study, but on a limited field of experience, and uncommon experience at that. I left school in 1914, when I was just eighteen ; during my longest period of service in France, with which this record is in the main concerned, I was nineteen. I had no period of manhood unsullied by war to serve as a standard of comparison ; and the life of the soldier after four years of war, and in the absence of any other experience, presented itself as the natural life of man.

These circumstances detract, I am well aware, from the value of the record here set out. If I had been rather older when the war came, if I had enjoyed years of manhood in a world at peace, I might have seen the war through different eyes. There are many others who have far greater qualifications to write about the war—men who saw more fighting, men who viewed the war through older and saner eyes, men with greater powers of literary expression. This record is subject to these and many other limitations ; I claim for it no quality other than fidelity. In the process of selecting what is worthy of record in my experiences I have not had in mind a case to prove, or a theory to advance. I have extenuated nothing. I have set down nothing in malice.

I well remember the fateful day on which we entered the war and the next day—the silence and depression of the former, when it seemed possible that our honour as a nation was compromised ; the relief and heartfelt thankfulness of the latter, when it became clear that whatever might befall us we could face the world united and undismayed. Rarely can a great nation have gone less willingly to war. Excitable people there no doubt were, who were overcome with their own eloquence and confused patriotism and jingoism in their disorderly minds. But of this there was no sign in the proceedings of the House of Commons, and *Hansard* for the first week of August 1914 is no ignoble record. Indeed we may be well content that posterity should judge us by that record, so free is it from any display of hate or slander, of arrogance or fear. Whether a firmer attitude at the outset would have prevented or postponed the war is a matter of doubt which can never be resolved; at least the policy pursued established beyond doubt our pacific intentions and brought us into the war a united nation.

The House of Commons can have witnessed few more splendid hours than that in which the leaders of all political parties gave their promise of unqualified support in all measures of national defence. Centuries before John Milton had described the scene in *Areopagitica* :

> Methinks I see in my mind a noble and puissant Nation rousing herself like a strong man after sleep, and shaking her invincible locks. Methinks I see her as an Eagle mewing her mighty youth.

England was not slow to answer. If there had been any hesitation, it was dissipated by the actions of the German army in Belgium. Feelings of generous emotion at the sufferings of a small and pacific nation supplemented the growing realisation that a menace to our national life existed which could be fought, not, as other wars, by a small professional army, but only by a nation in arms. The publication of the German Chancellor's speech to the Reichstag, " Necessity knows no law," and later of his interview with Sir Edward Goschen, established this conviction. When Sir Edward Goschen said that " Fear of consequences could hardly be regarded as an excuse for breaking solemn engagements," he spoke words which re-echoed through a nation whose chief pride has been that its word was its bond. Within a few weeks of the outbreak of war the Territorial Army had so far exceeded its complement that it had formed a second line, the first and second New Armies had been raised, and large contingents were on their way from the Dominions.

Serving first with a Territorial unit of the 51st (Highland) Division, which later won considerable fame in the Expeditionary Force and was known by the German army as the " devils in skirts," and afterwards with a New Army battalion of the Dorset Regiment, I had some opportunity of observing the spirit which animated the citizen armies in the early days of the war. Composed as they were of the most diverse types, inspired by a variety of motives, they had at least one universal characteristic, a determination to get as rapidly as possible to the war with a view to its early conclusion and their return to their usual avocations. Few of them professed any pleasure in the life of a soldier. They took soldiering intensely seriously, as a means to an end, in their hope of a rapid end. They well merited the description of their Saxon ancestors of fifteen hundred years before—" a martial but not a military people." The war was not a crusade in their eyes ; it was a disagreeable job which had to be seen through, however long it took and whatever sacrifice it entailed. It was clear to them that while solemn engagements could be broken at will on the plea of necessity, and while the most powerful military force ever known was under the control of men who held that view, the security of their country, and of all that it stood for in the way of ordered liberty, was subject to an intolerable menace. The greatest of contemporary writers watched my own regiment on the march with eyes which were not easily deceived. On September 5, 1914, the *Song of the Soldiers* told our story :

> What of the faith and fire within us,
> Men who march away
> Ere the barn-cocks say
> Night is growing gray,
> Leaving all that here can win us ;
> What of the faith and fire within us,
> Men who march away ?
>
> In our heart of hearts believing
> Victory crowns the just,
> And that braggarts must
> Surely bite the dust,
> Press we to the field ungrieving.
> In our heart of hearts believing
> Victory crowns the just.

Apart from these settled convictions, which were almost universal, the New Armies exhibited every form of diversity. There were men of every age, from every country, of every profession. The call to arms had sounded afar, and men long absent from their country took the first boat and hurried home. On my first night as a soldier I found myself with a schoolmaster from a remote township on the Amazon, two men just back from the Caspian Sea, and another from somewhere in Canada. Later I met men from much stranger places. Diversity of character was just as marked. We had, as every army has, our Bardolphs, our Pistols, and our Nyms. But the dominant type was perhaps the quiet-mannered, unassuming man, distinguished in days of peace chiefly by his pride in his profession or craft, and by his willingness to lend a hand when needed, a man very difficult to describe, but rather like Kent in *King Lear* or Horatio in *Hamlet*. There were also the simple-hearted and valiant, the natural leaders of their generation. Of them it is hard to speak. When Garibaldi, on the last day of the Roman Republic, summoned the citizens of Rome to follow him into unknown perils, rather than to surrender, he offered them " hunger, thirst, forced marches, battle, death. Let him who loves his country with his heart, and not with his lips, follow me." In no other spirit did many in the New Armies go to war. They had no words to express that which was in their hearts ; we are not an articulate people. If any soldier had delivered a speech on love of country, or the justice of our cause, consternation would have reigned among his comrades. These were matters which were taken for granted. But there was something in men's eyes which revealed more eloquently than words the faith that was in them, that faith of which W. E. Henley had sung many years before :

> Ever the faith endures,
>   England, my England !
> Take, and break us, we are yours,
>   England my own,
> Life is good and joy runs high
> Between English earth and sky,
> Death is death, but we shall die
> To the song on your bugles blown,
>   England,
> To the stars on your bugles blown !

I have few memories of the first year, except of the men with whom I served. My battalion of the New Army was quartered during the first winter in billets and later in a camp on the Great Heath of its native Dorset. In the early days there was every expectation that the battalion would proceed as a unit to France, but later it became a reserve battalion, and one by one the friends whom I had made were drafted to other battalions of the regiment in France and Gallipoli. This deprived the battalion of much of its early *esprit de corps*, and the long period of training became irksome. I experienced a great disappointment early in 1915, when it was discovered that I had attained the mature age of eighteen only in the late autumn of the year before. My name had been high in the list of subalterns ready for service at the front, and I had just missed a draft for Cape Helles. The inexorable decree of the War Office in regard to age was brought to my notice and my name was removed. For months I haunted the orderly room and in my bitter disappointment and my sure expectation of the early termination of the war contemplated the resignation of my commission and enlistment as a private soldier. I had observed that the affairs of the private soldier and more especially his age were not subjected to the same scrutiny as the affairs of the young officer. Birth certificates were not demanded, and age and youth met together within the happy years nineteen to thirty-five, which then entitled a man to the privilege of service in the field.

My enthusiasm would not have been of the same order if I had known that the great autumn offensive of 1915 would not end, as the uninstructed opinion of the subalterns' table firmly anticipated, in the Unter den Linden, but would eddy in a surf of blood round Loos and the Hohenzollern Redoubt. We little thought how much of hope and despair, of victory and defeat, lay before us, nor how weary was the road which ended at long last on the Rhine. We did not know how many milestones on that road must be passed, Loos, Somme, Ancre, Arras, Messines, Passchendaele, Cambrai, St. Quentin, Lys, before ever the great advance would begin, nor how few of us would be privileged to see the coming of victory.

The happy day at last arrived on which I was able to acquaint the Colonel that I could lay claim to the magic age of nineteen. I remember well the evening, a little later when, sitting at dinner, I heard a confusion of voices wishing me luck, my orders to join the 1st Dorset Regiment in the Expeditionary Force having arrived.

After the first few moments of excitement and pleasure that my turn for the great adventure had come at last, I looked round and a certain sadness came over me at the realisation that a chapter of my life was ended. These were the men who had been my companions in my first year of manhood; I was indebted to them for much. I had come to them shy and diffident; they had welcomed me and made me feel at home. Many of them had come from far afield, mature in experience; yet they had treated me as a comrade. In their company I had enjoyed much happiness. Not all the hours had been happy. In early days there had been difficulties and misadventures; latterly considerable monotony and tedium. There had been dark days on which friends left for Gallipoli and Flanders; and the nature of such leave-takings could hardly be in doubt at a time when the forlorn valour of the infantry was set in the scale against an immense superiority of technical equipment, and battalions were mowed down by machine guns as with a scythe on wire entanglements which the artillery had neither the guns nor the ammunition to cut.

But now that the time had come to leave I had only happy memories: the cool green woods emerald in the morning light, the long avenues aglow with rhododendrons, the illimitable peace of the great meadows by the river, the waves dancing in the sunlight on the golden beaches of Man of War Bay, the russet expanse of the limitless wasteland of the Great Heath tinged with fire in the rays of the setting sun, the eerie woods darkening in the twilight, the small and dismal copses on the hill-tops silhouetted against the evening sky, the road which stretched white in the light of the moon from Gallows Hill, the distant lights of the camp seen from afar. I remembered the happy hours of leave, the fine men I had met, the friends I had made. The next day the great moors of the South country, and the glades of the New Forest, seemed to me more than ever beautiful as the train bore me on my way to the mirk and mud of Flanders and the chill Unknown.

In my childhood I had often perused magazines in which the departure of troops for the front was depicted. It had seemed to me an occasion likely to give much satisfaction. Bands played. Crowds cheered. Generals shook private soldiers by the hand. The same troops on arrival in the field appeared also to have certain consolations. Battles undoubtedly were exhilarating affairs in which batteries came into action at the gallop and cavalry made gallant, and so far as could be judged, not too expensive charges. A degree of excitement clearly obtained which might mitigate any sense of inherent danger. I had already learned that there were no bands playing, nor colours flying, nor any panoply of war in modern battle; only the roar of the barrage, the deadly rat-tat-tat of machine guns, and a sea of reeking mud. I was not surprised, nor distressed, at the absence of ceremony at Victoria Station, nor the complete indifference of the population of Folkestone, who for more than a year had witnessed the daily passage of troops on leave and reinforcements to France and Flanders.

With two companions, officers of my own regiment, I presented myself at the Embarkation Office. We were told that we might spend the day in Folkestone and embark in the evening. This course clearly presented the danger that we might miss something of importance in France, and to the surprise of the Embarkation Officer we asked if we might go on the morning boat. The white cliffs of England gradually faded into the horizon, but I was not touched by solemn thought. The hour of action had begun. Well I knew that war was horrible; yet I was sure that it was still a great adventure. Light of heart I picked out the low outline of the French coast. Eagerly I talked of the Western Front with an officer of the Army Service Corps who modestly informed me that he knew nothing about it, and that the Military Cross which he wore had been won for great gallantry on the Rouen front. At last the ship passed through a slit in the long low shore and drew into the quay.

Evening found us at the great base camp at Etaples in a vast wilderness of tents and buildings. For mile on mile the camps stretched along the dunes. I was awed at the vast array which spoke of the growing might of the British Expeditionary Force. The night was spent in comfort. The camp was pitched on sand, wholly admirable in winter, as no amount of rain made any difference, but possessing the small defect that it found its unerring way into sleeping-bag, clothes, and hair. In the morning I rose early and drank in the splendid freshness of a winter dawn by the sea. I found myself in command of 150 men, and set out through the lines of camps, through some railway sidings and a wood, and then along a great road which stretched to the horizon as straight as only a French road can be. All around were hospital huts with hurrying orderlies and nurses, some in the uniform of the Red Cross, others in the grey of the territorials, a few in the green of a private hospital. Towards us the French women came to market, hatless and robust. Children crowded round, with apples clenched in their dirty little hands, crying in a monotonous sing-song, " Three apples—une pennee." Between the road and the sea, sheltered by a thicket of pine trees, was the cemetery marked already with long lines of wooden crosses.[1]

[1] The main line from the cross-Channel ports to Paris passes by this cemetery. It is the greatest of British War Cemeteries and is the last resting-place of more than 18,000 soldiers who died of wounds or sickness in the base hospitals.

We came to a chain of high sand dunes, on which many battalions of infantry were already drawn up.

The road had been crowded by line upon line of marching, whistling men. Now as they converged on the parade ground I realised that I was a unit of the great fighting force on the Continent, an officer in command of men. The sense of power in these disciplined battalions thrilled me; in it there was majesty, even splendour. This was the expression of a people's will. Every man of this great gathering was here of his own choice. This was the answer of a free people to a call-to-arms. This was England at war.

Already I recognised that life here was different from life at home. The machine, so great in size, recked little of the individual. This army, impressive in power, was also implacable. Men were finally dissociated from home ties. Here was no ordered civilisation with its sanctions and its safeguards. At home among the surroundings of happy and care-free years, it had been hard to realise the inexorable discipline which war demanded. Here in a new world a man dropped naturally into the habit of implicit and unquestioning obedience. He might grumble, but the job was done. The consequences of hesitation or disobedience were serious; they were death.

The training ground was the daily lot of subalterns at the base. I learned there something of various weapons, the machine gun and the bomb. The bombing instructor was a Scotchman with a strange, some might say a perverted, sense of humour. I learned also the art of building breastworks and digging trenches under the most favourable conditions, time being of no importance and the enemy conspicuous by their absence. In these model trenches old soldiers would wander in delight and merriment, inspecting the sunken wire, the revetted sides, the polished duck-boards, the wilderness of sand-bags. If we young soldiers had been sent for a walk in the mud-flats of the estuary of the local river, we would have derived a more accurate impression of the lot of the infantryman in the line.

Of that lot we heard much in the evenings from the veterans. It appeared that the front line was the most hilarious of places in which generals fell through duck-boards and re-appeared upside down, and jars of rum formed the most conspicuous feature of the landscape. In time a more than usually preposterous story would send us out laughing into the winter night to grope our way through the darkness to our tents. The censoring of letters was our only other occupation, and at first was interesting. The private soldier, finding himself at last at the war, and provided with unlimited paper at the canteens and huts of the Y.M.C.A. and other bodies, promptly wrote to a large circle of acquaintances. In their letters I saw for the first time a new world, with interests and standards of which I had previously no experience. Most of the letters were frank in a degree which surprised me. The world which I had known professed a hatred of sentiment, made a virtue of understatement, held in contempt anyone who in its expression " wore his heart on his sleeve." But I found the world of the private soldier wholly natural and without reserve. Most of the letters were homely and kind, bidding loved ones not to worry, sending kisses to the bairns, assuring anxious girls of fidelity and safety. A Highlander from Glasgow might in my opinion have benefited by the acquisition of some element of reserve. He had a faulty sense of humour which when dealing with incidents of his voyage across the Channel became tedious when repeated to a large circle of acquaintances. The less literary referred in opprobrious terms to the winter weather and the insipidity of French beer. The letters of a citizen of the United States who had joined the army after the sinking of the *Lusitania* were most interesting.

But my most vivid memory of the base is

an evening on the road which led from the training ground on the sand-dunes to the great camp. My company had been whistling various songs ; they began to whistle inadequately the Marseillaise. Between us and the sunset was a railway embankment, and silhouetted against the sky two French poilus in uniform. They turned on hearing the marching troops and sang in unison with them with a passion and a fervour which made a deep impression on all. In the light of evening with the great song ringing out over the sand-hills it seemed to me that for a moment I was privileged to apprehend that which was the soul of an indomitable nation, the glory that was France.

CHAPTER III

EARLY DAYS

AFTER a few days orders came. I was posted to the 1st Dorset Regiment, but for a time I was to undergo attachment to an Entrenching Battalion employed in digging a reserve line on the Somme. I accepted my fate with resignation, convinced that the digging of a reserve line must present greater reality than the tedious mock-warfare of the base and that I would be nearer to my regiment and to the front line over which still rested an aureole of glamour. I noted in my orders that " the *unexpected* portion of the day's ration " would accompany me.

The journey up the line was full of interest on this, the first occasion of making it. Midnight discovered me ploughing through wet sand in the darkness, laden with a variety of equipment, mostly useless. At Abbeville I was hastily bundled out, and after traversing a wilderness of railway lines, I found a hut in which I lay on a hard floor for the rest of the winter night. Towards dawn a stove was lit and a thaw set in. From time to time other stray subalterns arrived, decanted from passing trains, among them a new camp commandant for the local general. Before the war he had been in the Church; he was now a soldier. In the hours of that age-long night we became on terms of friendship; as so often in the war the friendship came to an end at dawn when we parted, he to the camp, I to the Somme.

For the first time I experienced the unforgettable coming of dawn at the front, white of face, unshaven, weary, an unpleasant taste in my mouth, my clothes all in the wrong place, a sensation akin to " pins and needles " everywhere. I experienced also that complete revulsion of feeling brought about by a bowl of tea, strong and sweet, but, alas! (for I was still on the Lines of Communication) without the rum which so improved its taste at dawn in the trenches.

Throughout the day the train jolted monotonously through Picardy and the featureless valley of the Somme. At Méricourt-Ribemont, the railhead, I was distressed to find the war still very distant. There were no guards posted, indeed no one appeared to be interested in the war, least of all in my arrival at it. I made inquiries as to my destination; I was advised to make it the canteen until something or somebody turned up. Accordingly I crossed the station-yard, crowded with lorries and ankle-deep in grey mud, to the canteen. There I remained until some outgoing officers arrived, who knew the whereabouts of my battalion. I hoisted myself on to a wagon beside the driver and set out for Henencourt.

It was a beautiful evening, and the countryside showed no sign of war. It might have been England, so quiet were the fields. The sun was setting. The countryside was aglow, serene, at peace. Yet beyond the dim, shattered tower of Albert Cathedral lay the grim uplands of the Somme battlefield. There two armies stood on guard, restless and watchful; there war brooded sullenly over the opposing lines, ready at any moment to break into fury. No doubt on this winter evening the countryside surrounding Longueval and Guillemont in the far distance was aglow with the same light, presented the same appearance of tranquillity and ordered peace. Within a few months those fields were destined to present a picture of infamy and desolation, without parallel in human experience, and the proud and passionate youth of three nations lay in battalions unburied in the thronging shell-holes.

The wagon rattled through a typical Somme village. Lath-and-plaster barns, mostly tumbledown and pocked with rat-holes, lined the road. Through narrow apertures in the barns could be seen courtyards noisome with vast heaps of accumulated manure, leaving only a narrow band of pavé at the edges as a means of access to the living-rooms beyond. Mongrel dogs, perpetually chained and half-savage through lack of exercise, were kennelled within the courtyards, and barked angrily at each passer-by. Leaving the village we passed a little cemetery thronged with metal crosses and florid monuments and through open fields, separated by no hedge or landmark, where old men and women were at work in the twilight. We came to Henencourt and drew up at the forge at the corner of the Millencourt—Albert Road. At the local presbytery, unoccupied owing to the absence of the priest on military service, I joined the subalterns of the Entrenching Battalion.

Everyone made me welcome. I was tired, lonely, and very shy, and the ready hospitality warmed my heart. I was destined to learn on many occasions afterwards that in this new world men having little yet had that little in common, and shared it with a grace and courtesy not often found in a prosperous and civilised community. By skilled rearrangement room was made for one more sleeping-bag on the overcrowded floor. Of furniture there was none, but the walls were adorned with the cheap sacred lithographs beloved of a Catholic peasantry, interspersed with the latest photographs of famous beauties torn from the illustrated papers. I rolled myself up in my bag, and at once fell asleep.

Early in the morning I heard the distant throb of guns. The sound went to my head, and I prevailed on another subaltern to accompany me to Albert in the hope that something might be happening in which we might become implicated. The subaltern was less interested; he had memories of Second Ypres and the German gas attack of April 1915, and regarded shell-fire with disfavour. But he remembered, no doubt, his early days of ignorance and enthusiasm, and consented to act as chaperon to my innocence.

Passing through Millencourt we came by way of a long winding road to the ridge on the western outskirts of Albert. On our left there was a large gun in fancy dress as a haystack. A loud clatter of falling masonry indicated that the German artillery was sending over a few light shells as we entered the town.

At this time the western side of the town had not been shelled in the same degree as the part which abutted on the Square and the La Boisselle—Bapaume Road. But every few houses showed gaping rents. At the corner where the great Amiens Road joined the Millencourt Road a great shell had laid open the drains under the road. Near by there lay exposed the ruins of a cycle factory, a mass of twisted girders and fallen masonry intermingled with frames and fittings piled in irremediable confusion and covered with dust. The Cathedral Square had been enlarged by the obliteration of the surrounding houses. Razed to the ground, their very existence might have been forgotten but for the cavernous cellars, half-choked with brick and rubble, which gaped below. Shell-holes gaped in the houses which still remained. From one a mattress hung precariously. The tower of the cathedral, surmounted by the gilt image of the Virgin and Child leaning downwards at a miraculous angle, stood erect though shattered and scored by countless shell-fragments. The tower was a favourite mark for the German guns, and I did not envy the lot of the military policemen on guard in its shadow. The cathedral walls were much battered, the roof had collapsed, the mosaics were littered pell-mell in a myriad fragments. The cathedral had never been a work of consummate art the destruction of which impoverished the world, as Ypres, Arras, and Rheims had been. Still it represented the love, labour, and devotion of many, who had worshipped here and were now homeless and far away.

We wandered through the streets to the Ancre, where smashed water-wheels lay in ruin, to the railway station, deserted and grass-grown. From time to time miners came by, sturdy and cheerful, covered with white chalk from head to foot, from their tour of duty at La Boisselle. There was also some infantry of the 18th Division, New Army battalions from the Eastern counties.

We hailed a passing limber, and in company with a wounded Tommy we returned to Henencourt. A limber has no springs and its shape is not adapted to the human form. The road was bad and the horses trotted nobly. Bruised and shaken I returned unromantically from my first visit to the war.

I awaited Sunday, a day of comparative leisure, with eager impatience. My regiment was reported to be in the neighbourhood, and I was determined to find it. I obtained possession of an army bicycle, an absurd and rickety machine, which had neither brakes nor bell. On it I made a laborious journey down the tree-lined road to Millencourt, and finding no Dorsets there, I moved off in the direction of Albert. On reaching the hill into the town I found, as I had anticipated, that the brakes were of no value. I passed a sentry at astonishing speed, skidded for several yards, and arrived with a thud in a large heap of French mud. If this had been composed of good Dorset heather mud, I should have been a hospital case. As it was French mud, compounded of glue and capable of holding a foot firmer than any vice, I merely stuck, and in time extricated myself without even a bruise. Proceeding more carefully into the town, I made inquiries which led me to suppose that the Dorsets were at Martinsart. My way led over the railway on to the Aveluy Road. On the right some troops were busy digging trenches and dug-outs in an embankment. As I passed the brick-stacks of the great Briqueterie a battery of guns barked suddenly, and some form of minor activity commenced, making me feel as if I really had reached the war at last. To the west and below the road lay a great expanse of water bounded by a high embankment. Beyond were the uplands on whose lower slopes our line ran. Trenches ran hither and thither, conspicuous by the white chalk of their parapets. I was soon in Aveluy, but could get no news of the Dorsets. My appearance when I reached home dishevelled and covered in mud made it clear that I would not have made a good impression on my regiment had I been successful in my search.

The short period which I spent with the Entrenching Battalion was not without value in my training as a soldier. I was at the age of nineteen in command of a company on active service and under conditions which did not facilitate the maintenance of discipline. The subaltern of the Regular Army had an easier task than the subaltern of the New Armies. The former came to a regiment of trained and disciplined soldiers, with high traditions. His authority was never open to question. He was supported by the experience of good non-commissioned officers; in the background there were senior officers able at all times to advise, and, if need be, to intervene with a view to preventing or remedying an error of tact or judgment. The New Army subaltern was thrown much more on his own resources. His senior officers had often as little experience of war as himself; his non-commissioned officers were chosen at the shortest of notice by methods of trial and error. His men came from every walk of life, wholly without military traditions and frankly scornful of discipline. In so far as they had any respect for his personal qualities, they were amenable to his authority. My company of the Entrenching Battalion was drawn from Glasgow, Liverpool, and the Durham minefields, places not usually credited with respect for discipline. I had, however, the great advantage of two excellent Territorial non-commissioned officers as sergeant-major and quartermaster-sergeant. The men often needed some management, but the harvest was worth the sowing, and I learned a little of the art of managing men.

Henencourt was dominated by a large château, owned by a very efficient member of the aristocracy. Here the staff, and my commanding officer, had comfortable quarters. The grounds were beautifully kept; avenues radiated through a great wood, converging on the château garden. The stable-yard was enormous and unspeakable. Part was used as stables, part had been converted into soldiers' baths, over which I had often to preside. A dovecot rose out of an enormous refuse-heap and a chain of filthy pools. There was also a large barn, in which concerts were held. The Highland Light Infantry provided most of the comic turns. I can still recollect with pleasure and amusement a young Highlander delivering a recruiting speech by the Prime Minister. No concert was complete without it, but I am afraid that both in matter and in manner it would have caused a sensation in England. A service was held in the barn on Sunday evening. The night was quiet, except for the incessant muttering of the distant guns. A few candles gave a flickering light. All round the barn men's equipment and rifles hung on the shadowed walls. The Communion Table was a rough wooden packing-case. Yet the service was impressive, had indeed a splendour often absent in more formal surroundings. Here the old prayers and hymns of far-off homes rose from men whose lives were forfeit of their own free will, while the guns throbbed a monotonous undertone.

The day gave me my first appreciation of the tedium of modern (and, I have little doubt, of ancient) war. For nearly eight hours a day I strolled up and down a hundred yards of sodden grass, watching the men dig. I realised that they were not digging in the manner prescribed by the Field Service Regulations, but I could not bring myself to tell a Durham miner, who had completed his task in much less than the scheduled time, that he knew nothing about digging and that I would show him the correct way. Later my miners were entrusted with the cutting of brushwood in a neighbouring wood, a task which diverted them exceedingly. I was able to warm myself in the wood by chopping branches. From time to time I conducted business by gesture with the local woodman. He was a veteran of 1870 and was prone to describe his part in that war, and the iniquities of the Germans, in a flood of patois which I could not understand. In the evening we returned across heavy ploughed fields and past a disused French cemetery overgrown with rank grass and redolent of decay to our parade ground, ankle-deep in mud, and our sodden tents.

The night was often spent in route-finding

in the dark. There were two guards to be turned out, late at night, one on the Millencourt—Albert road, the other in open country near Senlis. The first could be reached with some peril to life and limb by a ride of several miles in the dark on a bicycle which had no bell nor brake nor lamp. This was, however, preferable to a solitary walk, occupying too much of the night. The second guard was some two miles away. A deserted road leading to a mill made the first mile easy. Thereafter the route lay for a mile across ploughed fields, on a compass bearing, to a guard who was often a young soldier with a nervous touch on the trigger of his rifle. The rude hut where the guard lived was quite invisible at 100 yards on a dark night. It was surrounded by a network of trenches, into which it was very easy to blunder. Some skill was required to pick up the hut, as the only rough landmarks were a track, often ploughed over and lost, and a haystack on a cart road. Birds constantly rose out of the grass at one's feet with a great flapping of wings; in the glare of the lights from the opposing lines beyond the Ancre the ground changed suddenly from black to grey and then to black again; the wind swept over the bare wintry fields in uncanny whispers. It was a lonely and rather creepy journey, and at the time when I used to make it there was a shadowy franc-tireur who was reported to have shot at officers in a local wood. He probably did not exist, but it was quite easy to see him in a thousand shadows and weird forms which rose out of the darkness on the solitary four miles. I suppose that the orderly sergeant should have accompanied the orderly officer on these nocturnal rambles, but no one ever suggested it. Moreover it provided useful training for subsequent patrolling in No Man's Land. That this was not the professed object was, however, revealed some weeks after I left, as the nimble wit of an officer of high rank conceived the idea of placing a padlock on the hut, and the guard was adjudged no longer necessary.

Two expeditions relieved the monotony of my short period with the Entrenching Battalion. The first made me acquainted with the Ulster Division. I had charge of a draft of Royal Inniskilling Fusiliers. I marched with my Irishmen for some miles through the hilly countryside to Corps headquarters, then at Toutencourt. Here I made inquiries, but unfortunately entered the wrong room. I stood open-mouthed before a row of beautiful and confidential charts until I was discovered by a gunner and shown without ceremony to the door. My second attempt was more successful, and after inspection of my draft by a staff officer I was put into the hands of a very youthful subaltern of the Army Service Corps, who descended from a large car and interested himself in a number of London buses drawn up at the side of the road. I got up in front of the leading bus, and was enabled from this point of vantage to assess the pleasures and pains of a bus-driver's existence. Our bus had been designed to travel on the London roads; its performances on a wretched French cart track were at first funny and afterwards remarkable. If we were uncomfortable, we took good care to provide ourselves with comrades in misfortune. Every horse showed a desire to bolt, and we left behind us a trail of dust and of profane French and English. In the late afternoon I reported to the colonel of the Inniskillings, who insisted on my spending the night in the château where he was billeted, so that I had an excellent dinner and for the first time in France slept otherwise than on the floor. I found my way home through Amiens, and paid a visit to the Cathedral. I noted with interest the sand-bag walls which offered some small protection from the fate which had already overtaken Ypres and Rheims.

Returning I resumed the tedious routine, which was shortly broken by a minor operation directed by the Germans against Carnoy. The bombardment was heavy, judged by the standards of those days, and I was much impressed.

The houses in the village shook, and the roar of the guns reverberated over the countryside as in the heaviest of thunderstorms. In my ignorance I thought that Millencourt must be going up in the air and moved cautiously towards it in the hope of getting a better view. Arriving there I could find nothing unusual and passed through to the high ground by the Crucifix on the Albert road. It was a perfect winter evening; but the light of the setting sun in the west was matched by another and a savage light in the east. Round Albert livid flashes stabbed the sky. The trench lines were veiled in the smoke and dust of countless explosions. Albert was shrouded in a livid twilight. Over all a sense of impending doom brooded, majestic yet inexorable. I returned home with feelings of awe and wonder, and a few days later, reading the official communiqués, wondered whether the words "heavy bombardment" could not be elaborated so as to have a significance to those at home equal perhaps to one-hundredth part of the reality.

My second expedition took me far afield to the neighbourhood of Armentières. I had a draft of Durham Light Infantry. We marched to railhead, arriving some hours before the train was assembled. Then in the twilight we pursued the uneven tenor of our way down the valley of the Somme to Amiens. My Durhams were true to type, graced with an abundant good humour and an entire lack of self-consciousness. In the darkness of Amiens Station I overheard a conversation.

Chorus of Tommies : Alleyman no bon.
Porter : Hello.
Chorus : Alleyman no bon. Angleterre tray bon. Compree.
Porter : Hello. Compree. No bon.

The entente cordiale having been cemented by the offer of a tin of bully, the train moved forward to its inevitable destination, a siding in the railway wilderness of Abbeville. Again I found myself faced with a winter night, cold and sleepless, on the bare, inhospitable floor of a deserted hut. At five in the morning I was more than glad to receive orders to move. Having led an obstacle race over endless railway lines and railway trucks, I roused my sleepy Durhams, and, after some cross-talk between the Railway Transport Officers on duty, entrained. I collected as a companion a young Northumberland Fusilier, and together we heated one of Mr. Maconochie's excellent rations, which soon put a new complexion on the prospects for the day.

My companion had not wasted the opportunities offered by the war. He had been present as a dispatch rider at the battle of Mons, aged sixteen. In the retreat he had been wounded in the shoulder and had ridden his motor-bicycle to Paris with one hand. There he had spent his seventeenth birthday in hospital. On recovery he had joined the Northumberland Hussars and had taken part with them in the First Battle of Ypres, the first engagement of the Territorial Army. He had then been attached to the Scots Greys, but was invalided home. He received a commission in the Northumberland Fusiliers and came to France with the 50th (Northumbrian) Division, which was hurried straight into action on the occasion of the German gas attack which was the prelude to the Second Battle of Ypres. He was hit at once. Having now married and attained the age of eighteen, he was making his way again to Ypres.

At Fontenettes, outside Calais, the engine took a much-needed rest. I gathered that engines usually expired at this point, as there was a hut presided over by a fairy godmother, supplied with unheard-of delicacies, real tea and pâté-de-foie-gras sandwiches. The engine gathered strength and as the day advanced we attained St. Omer, then Hazebrouck, and in the late afternoon the railhead of Steenwerck, which was on the Belgian frontier behind Plugstreet Wood and Armentières.

It was four in the afternoon, and as it was Flanders, rain was coming down with a depressing regularity which foreboded a dirty evening. The men were tired and encumbered by heavy packs. The Railway Transport Officer told me that I need not go any farther, but I felt a certain obligation to accompany my draft to the end of their journey and I was buoyed up by the hope that fortune might so far favour me as to find the Durhams in the line.

It was a nightmare march. The guide, an orderly with a bicycle (I have distrusted all cyclists ever since), assured me that it was no distance. In my innocence I believed him. Our way led through Steenwerck town, where I learned the reaction of tired feet to Flanders pavé, and by a track, which might once have been a road, leading to the south. The track was unmetalled and had been churned into a sticky morass by ammunition columns and transport wagons. The mud washed round our ankles and made a burden of every step; at times single files alone could make any progress. In places great holes insufficiently filled with straw could be jumped one man at a time. We soon degenerated into a procession. Marching was not possible, as only at rare intervals could two men walk abreast. I inquired of the guide whether we were in sight of our destination, as the short distance which he had mentioned had been covered many times over. He made a vague sweep with his hand somewhere ahead. At last we reached a village. Was this it ? No. It was now growing late; for the first time I experienced the unmitigated gloom of a Flanders twilight. The rain descended without intermission. The appearance of the countryside suggested that it had been raining since the beginning of time. We were almost too tired to swear.

I halted and closed up the men, and finding some chocolate in a neighbouring cottage distributed it among them. We moved forward again. In front there were a few houses on a hill, surely they must be our destination. The guide was uncommunicative. We trudged our way up a small rise decked with trees silhouetted against the sky and came to a little village. The guide pointed to a vision of a promised land, which seemed miles away on the far horizon, and to a steeple. We dragged ourselves wearily forward through the mud; our movements had become mechanical, we had become almost indifferent. I had constantly to encourage and to assist my heavily burdened men. In this manner we came to a well-guarded bridge, and looked down, as for many centuries soldiers had done before us, on the muddy waters of the Lys.

It was dark when we passed through the next village; at the far end I halted so as to let the men close up. Where was battalion headquarters, I asked ? The guide answered blandly that we were not there yet ; it was some way on.

Then I spoke. I indicated in language which was excusable only in the circumstances what was my interpretation of the term " short distance " and what my frank opinion was of guides who defined the term otherwise than as I did. The guide was probably not impressed. A man who had served for some time as a guide in Flanders must have heard the English language at its most full and rich, and must have developed an absolute indifference to popular opinion.

The nightmare march continued through the mud and mirk, reinforced now by darkness. We halted outside a large farm. The adjutant of the Durhams emerged. In a moment my men had been taken away from me. I was led into the light and warmth of the farm buildings. Men sat round a great fire in the yard, with the flow of the light on their faces. The surrounding walls were in darkness. It was a scene typical of a hundred wars. Maybe in Marlborough's campaigns in Flanders this very farm-house had sheltered infantry soldiers as tired and as soaked as my little party.

The hospitality of the Northern Counties is proverbial ; the hospitality of the front is a memory of the war which still has power to warm the heart of the soldier. Much he would wish to forget, but not that gracious memory. I found myself the guest of a North Country battalion at the front. My wet clothes were taken from me and sent to the farm kitchen to dry. Socks and slippers were immediately forthcoming. The commanding officer found me one thing, the adjutant another. I was soon arrayed in a complete set of dry clothes contributed by every officer in the mess. I did not find out till later that the battalion was relieving trenches the next evening and would want all the dry clothing which they had. The major filled me with whisky and soda. Dinner arrived. The company was excellent. The glow of the fire in the great fireplace of the farm warmed me until I had forgotten the mud, the cold and the exposure of the preceding hours. The outlook became more than bright, and I retired to a straw-covered shelf in a barn well content to enjoy, notwithstanding the cold, a night of untroubled sleep.

The morning passed in a discussion of the best means of taking prisoner a German known to be resident in an exposed sap. Meanwhile, desultory shelling went on in the vicinity. During lunch a heavy battery ranged on a farm a hundred yards away and made a direct hit. The next shell fell between us and the farm, and it seemed clear that the battery would not fail to score another direct hit, and this time on our farm, within a few minutes. The major looked out of the window, ordered all the men into the cellar, and helped himself to a whisky-and-soda. The atmosphere grew a little tense. The major helped me to some rice pudding.

Fate ordained, however, that the battery should cease fire at that precise moment. Possibly the German lunch hour had arrived. The hand of death was stayed at the neighbouring farm, to which the doctor was at once called away. It was littered with dead and wounded men and horses.

In the afternoon I set out again for Steenwerck, viewing with more friendly eyes a countryside less gloomy than it had seemed the evening before. As I walked down the road a concealed battery opened fire a few yards in front of me with a succession of vivid flashes. For a moment I thought that they could not have seen me and was tempted to take cover before the next round. Fortunately for my dignity I realised in time that their line of fire could not but be parallel to the road, not across it. Arriving at Steenwerck I met a subaltern of the Cameron Highlanders who had been with his regiment since 1914, and had missed one battle only, Loos, the most recent. He was attending to his horse, which had a perverse objection to windmills and had just seen one on the road from Plugstreet Wood. The subaltern had been billeted in early days at a farm near by. We went there, and received a noble welcome, common enough no doubt in the early days of the war, but now in the second winter less often to be found. My companion spoke perfect French and was very much at home. The younger generation produced coffee, beer, and unlimited bread, butter, and eggs. Whenever our glasses of beer showed any sign of diminishing, they were at once filled to the brim again. My command of the language was insufficient to enable me to say that I did not like French beer, and I doubt whether I would have had the heart to say it. The older generations disappeared into the haze of the chimney corner. I picked out grandfather and grandmother, and I thought that great-grandmother was dimly discernible beyond. We left after exchanging many expressions of goodwill.

The train groaned slowly to Calais, where we descended. In the ensuing mêlée I missed the Cameron Highlander, who was searching for the Paris express, as he had a few days' Paris leave. I found the express and inserted myself in a carriage full of French and Belgian officers. I remember two of them embracing each other as I sat down, but I was already half asleep and the subsequent journey through France interested me no more. When I reached Henencourt after a four-mile walk in the early morning I was still rather tired. I had a splendid plan. I would not report to the orderly room to-day, but would have a good sleep. The next day I would report. On the third I would start work again. But my luck was not in. My old billet was deserted ; my friends had gone. I received orders to depart within two hours to join the 1st Battalion of the Dorset Regiment. The dream of many months of arduous training had been fulfilled.

CHAPTER IV

THE DORSET REGIMENT

AFTER a short journey on a wagon I was deposited with my kit in a village reputed to be occupied by my regiment. I soon ascertained that they had left earlier in the day for a village ten miles away. The quartermaster was known to be somewhere, but no one could find him. I had nowhere to go and had not yet learned the art of making myself at home in unpromising surroundings. For hours I wandered round the village feeling very conspicuous, and reading, until I almost knew them by heart, the dull notices on the door of the church. When at length I met the quartermaster, I found a lively altercation in progress. The interpreter, a shy and inoffensive young man, was endeavouring to reconcile his obvious sympathy with his fellow-countrymen with the demands, emphatically expressed, of the quartermaster for a large number of wagons to convey the battalion blankets. The Army Service Corps lorries were so much behind time that unless transport was immediately forthcoming, the whole regiment would spend a very cold night. The interpreter agreed ; the inhabitants of the village did not. To the undisguised relief of the interpreter the arrival of the lorries led to an amicable solution of the difficulty.

The quartermaster, W. Alderman, with whom I now became acquainted, was a Dorset soldier of long service. The regiment represented his world. He had no desire to look beyond it. His life had been spent in its service ; its welfare was his welfare, its reputation the only thing which mattered. He held that the regiment had a right, possibly a prior right, to anything which the army chose to supply to the troops in the way of food and small comforts. He had no difficulty in establishing the right, as there was hardly an officer, quartermaster, or non-commissioned officer concerned with supplies whom he had not met during his long service at home and in India. The small residue whom he had not met soon became subject to his moral ascendancy.

He became quartermaster shortly after the battle of the Marne. Thereafter he made a point of accompanying the rations to their destination, wherever it might be, in battle, in trenches, or on the march. It was in his view his duty, and no one else could do it for him. For four years he rode at the head of his wagons over roads constantly searched by the enemy guns, and led his ration parties up the communication trenches or over the battlefield to battalion headquarters. It was a matter for wonder that he survived so long; his disregard for danger was absolute. He died in one of the last battles of the war, at the head of his transport on the road. I am glad that he lived to take part in the march of victory and to add to his ribbons that of the Military Cross.

An evening journey across the rolling uplands of Picardy, bathed in the splendour of a winter sunset, brought us to a large village encircled by trees. I found that the mess was in the house of the curé behind the church. The curé himself, very genial, was still in residence. Dinner, more than welcome after a long day, followed. Feeling most conspicuous I took my place at the table. I met for the first time Robin Kestell-Cornish, who became my greatest friend.

I had hopes that I might be posted to B Company, since my uncle had been killed in command of it at the battle of the Marne. The adjutant, H. C. Butcher, had the same idea. The evening, however, passed in much merriment, and at its conclusion I was taken in charge by Robin Kestell-Cornish, who held the command of A Company. He said that he wanted me with his company, and that he would make it all right with the adjutant in the morning. I thought this more than likely, having observed that they were on the best of terms. It was always difficult to refuse anything to Kestell-Cornish, and with A Company I remained.

We groped our way in the dark to company headquarters, where I met the company sergeant-major and quartermaster-sergeant, Jim Miller and Cannings. They were both non-commissioned officers of the " old contemptibles " and had been continuously with the regiment since the battle of Mons. Both wore the ribbon of the Distinguished Conduct Medal. Cannings had been groom to my uncle, and the discovery that I had this connection with the regiment gave me at once a place in their regard. Steps were at once taken to get me a servant and the name of Private Thomas Chapman was mentioned. An orderly was sent to rouse him. Soon he arrived, sleepy and blinking in the glare of the candle-light. He had served with the Sherwood Foresters in South Africa; at the age of forty-six he had joined up again. Already he had served for nine months with his platoon, refusing to be a servant or to accept any job which might take him off duty in the front line. It was counted to me for righteousness that he consented to be my servant. While he was with me I heard no word of censure or complaint pass his lips, no matter how trying the circumstances. He was more to me than a servant, he was a most loyal friend.

Good fortune attended me that evening. In the four men whom I had now met, and with whom I was destined to grow to manhood through trials and hazards most capable of revealing the best and the worst in man, I had been privileged to find the professional soldier at his best.

I was more than pleased to find myself with the Regular Army, since my family had been connected with the fighting services for many generations, and with the 1st Battalion of my regiment, whose fortunes I had followed with interest throughout the war. I came to a Regular regiment with a considerable predisposition towards the professional soldier. This predisposition became admiration during my period of service in the field. I feel able to put on record my admiration, inasmuch as I was not, and never became, a professional soldier.

To the "services" the early battles of the war are the familiar names: Mons, Marne, Aisne, First and Second Ypres, Neuve Chapelle, Festubert. In these battles the Regular Army guarded the awaking of England and in the act ceased to be.

The casualty lists, not so long as in the later battles, were more grievous to that small section of the community which gave to the Army its officers. The "services" constitute a small world, in which everyone at some time or other is bound to meet. Never a casualty list was published in the first year of the war but there was in it the name of an acquaintance, if not of a friend; in the autumn of 1914, and the spring of 1915, the regular soldier might well doubt, in reading the lists, whether in certain regiments any officer had survived. I well remember the first list, which darkened one evening on Salisbury Plain. A few days later another list contained an all too familiar name.

During my period of service with the 1st Battalion of my regiment I learned to admire the qualities of the Army which took the field in August of 1914. These qualities are commonly overlooked, except in time of war. The Regular Army is not in the habit of singing its own praises. It has no publicity department. It is singularly impervious to praise or blame. It was not seriously disturbed by the criticisms levelled against it by excited politicians many years ago; indeed, a soldier still refers affectionately to other soldiers as "the brutal and licentious" in commemoration of an historic speech during the Boer War. In the same spirit the soldier welcomed the reference by the " All Highest " to " Sir John French's contemptible little army," and was proud to be known by that title. He was embarrassed rather than flattered by the change from detraction to appreciation which succeeded the outbreak of war. In his own view he had been in no need of apology in peace; he felt in less need of approbation in war. He had his traditions; of these the principal was that a man should " go out without a word." In the early battles of the war he was not false to that tradition, and no body of men have a greater claim to the splendid epitaph in Ecclesiasticus :

And some there be which have no memorial.

A body of men who obey this tradition must expect to be the subject of misrepresentation. Generals are accused of lack of imagination in the conduct of major operations by men who have never demonstrated their ability to command a platoon on a field day. The soldier is accused of bartering away his right to determine his own conduct, of having no creed, no will of his own.[1] He is a " mer-

[1] Most eloquently in *Revolt in the Desert*, p. 422 :
" And it came upon me freshly how the secret of uniform was to make a crowd solid, dignified, impersonal ; to give it the singleness and tautness of an upstanding man. This death's livery, which walled its bearers from ordinary

cenary," and is so described in terms of depreciation by men who in the conduct of a successful business have evidently been inspired by no mercenary motive, but by a spirit of service to the community. There is no reply. The counsel for the prosecution has his say; there is no counsel for the defence.

Of the conduct of the war by the higher command I have no qualification to speak. But in reading much of the criticism which has been levelled against the "war of attrition" and the "wearing-out battle," and the brilliant expedients which in the opinion of the critics might have re-established a war of manœuvre and evaded the need of frontal attack, I have sometimes wondered whether anything short of a breakdown in German morale would ever have taken us to the Rhine, and whether that breakdown could have been accomplished by any other means than the hard pounding which the German army always expected, and obtained, in their battles against the British Army, however small the territory gained.

life, was sign that they had sold their wills and bodies to the State: and contracted themselves into a service not the less abject for that its beginning was voluntary. Some of them had obeyed the instinct of lawlessness: some were hungry: others thirsted for glamour, for the supposed colour of a military life: but, of them all, those only received satisfaction who had sought to degrade themselves, for to the peace eye they were below humanity."

Of the soldier's creed I have greater qualifications to speak, as the occasions are many when I have observed that creed under trial. The soldier has not bartered away his right to his private judgment; he has renounced it—a very different thing. Renunciation is a quality much in disrepute, since modern education set out to teach the virtues of self-expression. But the need for it is no less great; indeed, the more one part of the community achieves self-expression, the more must the other part of the community renounce. Fortunately renunciation has its rewards: in time of peace the soldier learns that in putting the interests of his regiment ever before his own interests he obtains a greater freedom, not a less; in time of war the soldier may gain that sense which has been described by Bernard Shaw as the true joy of life, the sense of " being used for a purpose recognised by yourself as a mighty one."

The soldier, moreover, does not object to the title of " mercenary." In a world in which the word " service " is on everyone's lips, the contribution made by professional pride to the welfare of the community is apt to be overlooked.

The soldier saw during the war disinterested service rendered by men who had never heard the word and were wholly unconscious of noble motives. He saw on occasion that a capacity to express idealism is not always accompanied by a willingness or an ability to practise it. He learned to respect the less vocal part of the community on whom the burden of its support mainly rests. For my own part I often think that the advancement of civilisation, and the growth of social consciousness, have been due more to professional pride than to the eloquence of the enthusiast. In war it was my experience that the most reliable troops were those whose morale derived from pride in their profession and in the traditions of their regiment; in peace I have found that the most valuable companions in an enterprise are the men who are too proud to be associated with a failure. Idealism takes so much out of people that the reaction is strong; pride may never reach such heights, but it lasts longer, and in war the army which wins is the army which stays the course.

"Pride" is a word which has many meanings; the pride of the Regular Army had in it nothing of arrogance. The sense in which I have used the word is that of moral force, and this moral force was built up of certain qualities taught to the young soldier.

They are set out in Sir John Fortescue's admirable handbook on *Military History*, published early in 1914:

Self-reverence, which can be based only upon high aspirations and high ideals; self-knowledge, which combines the courage to face facts, the patience to accept them, the constancy to turn them to good account; self-control, the offspring of self-denial and self-discipline. We are too much inclined to think of war as a matter of combats, demanding above all things physical courage. It is really a matter of fasting and thirsting; of toiling and waking; of lacking and enduring; which demands above all things moral courage.

It was by the exhibition of these qualities that the Regular Army maintained its morale in the long rear-guard action on the pitiless road from Mons to the Marne, and grimly enduring held the line from Ypres to La Bassée, against continuous onslaught by greatly superior forces in October and November of 1914, until regiments were reduced to companies and ultimately to platoons.

I have no wish to depict the professional soldier in terms of romance. He regards himself in no such light. I have been at pains only to show that he has something which is commonly denied to him—a creed. The dead of 1914 " went out without a word " in accordance with their traditions; they rest content under the splendid epitaph of A. E. Housman:

> These, in the day when heaven was falling,
> The hour when earth's foundations fled,
> Followed their mercenary calling
> And took their wages and are dead.

The village of Rainneville, at which I joined my regiment, was far behind the lines and not overcrowded. I had a good billet on the Amiens road. The old lady who was my hostess was friendly and full, perhaps too full, of gossip, to which I replied haltingly in broken French. Her son was at Verdun, then a quiet sector, and had recently been home on leave. She used to show me his photograph with much pride. I thought of her later when the great attack on Verdun overran the French forward lines. She had a particular affection for the Scotch, and talked to me of a Highland regiment and a certain officer who had promised to visit her in a motor-car after the war. I think next to the safe return of her son she valued this promise more than anything else.

No sooner had we settled in this comfortable village than a rumour came through that the regiment was destined to form a training school for officers and non-commissioned officers of the 32nd Division, lately arrived in France, and would move for that purpose to Frechencourt. I was utterly disgusted, as I had no other ambition at that time than to arrive at the earliest possible moment at the war. For months I had conspired to get to France ; now that I was there one incident after another occurred to stand in my way. I had, in the event, not long to wait.

The rumour was confirmed, and we took to the road. The rain beat down on us till we were soaked to the skin. The road was abominable, as indeed were most roads on the Western Front at this time, when the Higher Command had not more than enough men to hold the line. Later pioneer and labour battalions became numerous; officers with professional qualifications were detached for duties for which they were specially fitted, and the war in the back area underwent a process of cleaning up. The road was bad in itself and was blocked by lorries which had stuck. The column of march was checked; the rear companies were left far behind. Arriving at Frechencourt I saw my company to their quarters in barns at the top of the village and then viewed with disfavour the corner of a tiny room in the empty school-house which had been allotted to me as a billet. Soon, however, the atmosphere brightened. Chapman, my servant, was an old soldier. My valise appeared and with it a change of clothing. A biscuit tin, heaped with charcoal, improved the outlook, if not the atmosphere.

Here I often lay in my sleeping-bag on the floor reading by the light of a candle. I had brought with me to France *The Dolly Dialogues*. I was not the only officer of the regiment who found in them the needed diversion from the harsh verities of war. It was good to live for an hour in a world which had existed but yesterday, a world of the infinitely trivial, the wholly artificial, from which we had reverted into another and earlier world, primitive and barbarous, yet perhaps nobler and more sincere. Later I acquired two more books, a novel of Rider Haggard and *The Oxford Book of English Verse*. The former I found in the front line near Authuille, and read during a quiet spell of trench warfare, wondering the while how the hazards undergone by the hero of the novel could be accounted exciting, seeing how much greater were those afforded daily to the infantry subaltern in the line. The latter arrived in an inauspicious hour, but surviving it travelled with me north to the Belgian coast and south to Italy.

We were at Frechencourt for a short time only, as developments at the front caused a change of plan, greatly to my satisfaction. My feeling was not shared by others; a month later I felt exactly as they did about trench warfare. In the meantime we trained in the mornings in an orchard at the bottom of the valley below the château, which was approached by the muddiest of tracks. Sometimes we went for a march, generally up a hill from which a splendid view could be obtained. Often on clear winter mornings we manœuvred on the terraces of the hill until lunch time, and as we marched home up the village street, we were chiefly concerned in wondering to whom victory would go in the platoon football match in the afternoon.

A brigade route-march made a great impression on my mind. Our route led along one of the great poplar-lined roads of France, which run straight as a die for league after league. When the road dipped, the line of battalions stretched from horizon to horizon. We seemed a great and formidable force, yet we were but a brigade, one of a hundred or more in France at that time. We passed through Querrieu, later Army Headquarters; the cockney element in the regiment found the naming of the streets hard to follow. It was reasonable that having passed down Shaftesbury Avenue we should find ourselves in Oxford Street; but it was most improper that we should then pass in rapid succession Cannon Street, Charing Cross Road, and Lombard Street, where the Field Cashier lived. In the evening we returned home by a little stream which recalled a hundred memories of England.

The weather broke. There was a heavy fall of snow and hail. The post lorry was snowed up. The streets were deep in snow. All was still. The houses were mantled in white. The pathways were dumb. Frechencourt was transformed as in a fairy tale from its natural squalor into a village of dreams. Kestell-Cornish, the padre, and I indulged in tobogganing on the battalion dixie carriers in a disused chalk-pit at the foot of the village and inveigled other and senior officers into the pastime, to their great discomfort.

The mess was in the château at the top of the village. The furniture was scarce, but there were two rooms of fair size. These quarters were considered luxurious by those who had long been accustomed to regard themselves as fortunate if they found so much as the bar of an estaminet for mess purposes in the villages in the vicinity of the line. Here I became intimate with a body of men whose memory I shall honour so long as life lasts.

The hand of death lay heavy on that company. To my certain knowledge fourteen, nearly one-half, gave their lives, and of the remainder I do not know the fate of several. The conditions under which the war was carried on decreed that those fourteen numbered most of the best-loved, the gallant and single-hearted. They sleep, many of them, on the uplands of Picardy. They asked for no reward, no sunlit fields of heaven. They played a man's part, and held their heads high, till Death came in a roaring whirlwind and one more little hour was played. Yet perhaps, as they sleep, they hear a voice across the ages " Well done."

The shadow which lay athwart the lives of all could not be discerned in the mess. Sometimes on a walk, or in the solitude of a billet or dugout, a man might unburden his soul to another. Once I went for a walk with a subaltern, one of my contemporaries at Rugby, whom I had always regarded as among the most cheerful and care-free of my friends. I was surprised when he told me that life meant nothing to him, that he had hardly known a happy hour, that he cared very little whether he lived or died. Being very young, I had not previously realised how much of unhappiness the laughter of a brave man may conceal. Death waited for this subaltern on the Somme. He kept his rendezvous without flinching and without dismay. He did not apprehend the majesty, or recognise the dominion, of Death. To him, as to the Guards Ensign in *The Way of Revelation*, Death gave not a summons, but a welcome, " arms wide to embrace, sleep strong to enfold, a friend there faithful and true."

A man often seemed to know when his end was near; and the knowledge of it was written in his eyes. A power to apprehend danger is instinct in men living under primitive conditions; our conditions were worse than primitive and that power was highly developed.

But whatever a man's inner feelings, he had a duty to make life as tolerable as conditions allowed for his neighbours. His heart might be cold and sick within him; but he did not ask others to share his sorrows. The mess at Frechencourt was no doubt typical of a thousand messes in France. I remember night by night a line of merry faces, the constant good-humour and laughter. It may be that the laughter was born of defiance rather than innate happiness. But I think that it was real and was derived from a sense of high fellowship, the greatest reward of a soldier's life and creed.

I am grateful to that benevolent fortune which gave me, all unworthy, the privilege of membership of so gallant a body of men, of a company which merited the proud title of " gentlemen unafraid."

CHAPTER V

WINTER ON THE SOMME

OUR brief stay at Frechencourt soon ended, and we set our faces to the east, towards the trench lines on the Somme. In a blinding snowstorm we marched heavily laden for the last time down the village street, and up the hill. On reaching the summit of the hill we became exposed to the full force of the storm which swept over us in white fury straight from the north. The left flank of the battalion was covered with freezing snow, which caused much ear-trouble and cost A Company one of its officers, who was invalided to England. At first I was very miserable, but was cheered by the company of Kestell-Cornish and the men. If we had experienced a shower, everyone would have grumbled. A storm, however, was sufficiently serious to be treated as a jest. The men marched uncomplaining; from time to time a song would be taken up or a joke passed down. Soon I caught the infection of the prevailing hilarity. Chapman, my servant, marched behind me, silent and unperturbed.

Our first halt left A Company in an exposed

WINTER ON THE SOMME

position on a hill. We were glad when it ended. A blizzard is more tolerable when one is moving. An aerodrome then caused us much trouble; the heavy lorries covered half of the road. We were reduced to marching in single file, and the line of march was wholly disorganised. A Company, being the last company, got the full benefit of the disorganisation and lost the services of the band. By the time that we reached Henencourt the snow had abated. We marched through, as if on parade, so that the assembled crowd, composed of other regiments, might appreciate that the Dorset Regiment did not notice snowstorms and had never heard of fatigue. We came to Millencourt; my men were soon billeted. Here we were in reserve. The 2nd Manchesters had gone on to La Boisselle. The 14th Infantry Brigade was again in the line.

At Millencourt I learned something of the reputation of the La Boisselle trenches. They were among the most notorious in the British lines. For a considerable distance the opposing lines were divided only by the breadth of the mine craters: the British posts lay in the lips of the craters protected by thin layers of sandbags and within bombing distance of the German posts; the approaches to the posts were shallow and waterlogged trenches far below the level of the German lines, and therefore under continuous observation and accurate fire by snipers. Minenwerfer bombs of the heaviest type exploded day and night on these approaches with an all-shattering roar. The communication trenches were in fact worse than the posts in the mine craters to most people; there were, however, some who always felt a certain dislike of sitting for long hours of idleness on the top of mines which might at any moment explode. In the craters movement of any kind in the daytime was not encouraged.

The four company commanders and the colonel went up to examine the trenches and reported on them unfavourably. The colonel stated that in his long experience they were the worst trenches which he had ever seen. Nobody, however, seemed either excited or depressed. In fact, stories of mud up to the thighs and Minenwerfer unlimited appeared to constitute a good joke with the regiment.

One evening a service was held in a little, grubby, candle-lit room in the mayor's house. The next afternoon we left Millencourt. My company was the last to start, as we were taking over Usna Redoubt, a strong point in the support line. We marched through Albert, over the railway bridge, past the ruined cycle factory, and so through the square under the shadow of the shell-torn church, with the image of the Virgin and Child dependent at a miraculous angle from the tower, and out on to the Bapaume Road. At the light-railway crossing beyond the town we halted again under a great calvary to inquire for some promised gum-boots, which were unhappily not forthcoming. The railway line was overgrown with weeds; in happier days little trains had puffed along it to Péronne through a countryside which had no history, through Fricourt, Mametz, Montauban, Bernafay, and Trônes Wood, and so to Guillemont and Combles. On our right were the remains of a house, whose shelter looked most inviting, and a battery of artillery, well concealed, in action. We proceeded slowly up a long and unpleasantly exposed stretch of broad *route nationale*, which extended bleak and haunted to the skyline. On one side were shelters scooped out of the bank, and some dug-outs where the tunnelling company, working in the mines of La Boisselle, kept their stores. The road was under constant shell fire, but was protected from direct observation from the German lines by a rise on the summit of which were the riven trunks of five tall trees. Some telegraph posts, still erect, represented the only other feature of the landscape. We entered the communication trench and halted for a moment. I took the opportunity of looking round up the mournful overgrown road, protected by a wire barrier, beyond which no traffic had passed for many months, and down to the Ancre and Albert city behind us. Then we moved forward down a good and fairly dry trench, turned down one much worse and very shallow, and so arrived in Usna Redoubt, a maze of well-constructed trenches and deep dug-outs, in one of which I found the outgoing officers endeavouring to leave us a respectable fire by pouring rum on to the stove, a strange initiation into the practices of trench warfare.

The night was peaceful in Usna Redoubt; the shelling, which was heavy on our front line, and the snow, which fell through the night, did not disturb our sleep. Dawn came, and I set out to explore the neighbourhood. Growing tired of the mud and constant traverses of the communication trench, I took advantage of a fold in the ground which denied direct observation from La Boisselle and emerged into the open. I came to a grave with a black cross, marked "Deux Soldats français morts pour la Patrie." The grave, isolate amid the sullen waste of the battlefield, appeared strange, almost uncanny; the rank grass whispered sadly in the fresh morning breeze.

In the valley below was Aveluy, bathed in the freshness of sunrise. To the north was Authuille Wood, on whose eastern edge our line ran, where my regiment was almost annihilated a few months later. Beyond it lay the great mass of Aveluy Wood. Through a gap could be seen the uplands beyond the Ancre, with the ruined villages of Hamel on our side and Beaumont-Hamel on the German. I turned to the west. Below lay Albert and in the background Millencourt; smoke curled from the chimneys, forming a blue haze amid the tall trees. I looked at the village which I had left the day before as from another world. I reflected that in the five miles which lay between were a thousand years of civilisation and all " the ages' slow-bought gain." There man went forth to his labour until the evening; here he toiled unceasingly to maim and to slay. Here Death held sway, and the life of man was numbered in days, not years. And Death was no " sundown, pleasant and serene," but a stroke as of lightning, or a long-drawn-out agony, suffered alone amid all the grim fury and horror of battle. There man lived in some measure of comfort and security; here he lived in noisome holes burrowed out of the earth, as primitive man had lived in forgotten ages, and, as then, his every artifice was employed to keep alive the torch of life. There a thousand little fussy things mattered, but here the conventions and disguises of civilisation were laid aside and the real man was seen. The worries and cares of the old life had lost their power, for man was face to face, every hour, with the eternal riddle of death.

It was the quiet hour after dawn, and for the moment there was peace. Not a shot rang out to break the stillness. Yet many were watching the last dawn stealing over these chalk uplands; the regiment before Authuille lost sixty-six men that night.

I turned back from the grave of the French soldiers and made my way to Usna Redoubt. The morning was peaceful. In the afternoon I and a companion went forward to inspect the mine craters, which my company was to take over in the course of the night. We passed down our front-line trench towards the ruins of the cemetery through which our line ran. East of the cemetery was the heaped white chalk of several mine craters. Above them lay the shattered tree stumps and litter of brick which had once been the village of La Boisselle. We progressed slowly down the remains of a trench and came to the craters, and the saps which ran between them. Here there was no trench, only sand-bags, one layer thick, and about two feet above the top of the all-prevailing mud. The correct posture to adopt in such circumstances is difficult to determine; we at any rate were not correct in our judgment, as we attracted the unwelcome attentions of a sniper, whose well-aimed shots experienced no difficulty in passing through the sandbags. We crawled away and came in time to a trench behind the cemetery, known as Gowrie Street. Liquid slime washed over and above our knees; tree trunks riven into strange shapes lay over and alongside the trench. The wintry day threw a greyness over all. The shattered crosses of the cemetery lay at every angle about the torn graves, while one cross, still erect by some miracle, overlooked the craters and the ruins of La Boisselle. The trenches were alive with men, but no sign of life appeared over the surface of the ground. Even the grass was withered by the fumes of high explosive. Death, indeed, was emperor here.

We plodded slowly through the mud, and became jammed owing to a party making their way in the opposite direction. An intermittent bombardment was going on. So attuned is human nature in such surroundings to the presence of danger that we all became aware at the same moment that a Minenwerfer bomb had been projected directly at us. It rose high in the air, and I for one, and I think the others too, as we watched its flight, were certain that it would land directly on us and blow us to pieces. Nothing is so destructive as a Minenwerfer bomb which hits its mark; indeed, a man becomes as though he had never been born. I watched it, stupefied rather than afraid. Movement was impossible in the liquid mud. There was a swish over our heads ; the bomb just cleared the trench and exploded with a deafening crash above us. The danger past, I felt rather weak for a moment. We disentangled the two parties and passed on, meeting an officer of a trench mortar battery whose intervention we invited. He was an amusing person, and perhaps owing to that circumstance we did not observe another Minenwerfer bomb till a man fell off the firestep of the trench with commendable speed. This bomb had been aimed with greater accuracy, and fell right into the trench. It would have killed several of us but for the happy circumstance that it failed to explode. In due course we came to " Burnt island " —so named, as indeed were all the trenches in this sector, by the 51st (Highland) Division which had taken them over from the French —and so home to Usna Redoubt.

My company was not due to take over the front line till the later part of the night, and I endeavoured to obtain a little sleep. In this I met with no success, as a raid took place near Authuille. All the guns for miles on each side joined in the bombardment. From horizon to horizon the Somme battlefield was ablaze with a lurid light. The air was shrill with the passing of countless projectiles, the lighter shells whispering, the heavier shells throbbing, the heaviest roaring with the noise of express trains racing into eternity. The ground shook with the all-shattering explosions. Above all brooded a sense of awful power, instinct at once in the appalling majesty of the thundering guns, and in the undaunted spirit of the watchers along the trench lines, undismayed in the face of the twin terrors of darkness and eternity.

At two in the morning came the order to move. Two is not an hour of the night at which I normally feel at my best, but unhappily during the war it was quite a usual hour for relieving trenches. I became happier when we moved off. We came to Dunfermline Avenue, where the mud was so deep that I was constrained to warn my neighbours against the danger of submarines. In due course I took over Trench 121, which lay to the left of the craters and was the normal approach to them. The outgoing company was undisguisedly glad to be off, and provided lurid tales of the events of the preceding thirty-six hours. My most vivid memory of the night is that of two very old soldiers, whose home address was well east of Aldgate Pump, addressing the German army in familiar, if deplorable, language ; while a machine gun swept the parapet of the trench from end to end their heads remained silhouetted against the skyline, and, so far as I could see, did not move up or down during the two hours of their watch.

My platoon, which was No. 1 Platoon of A Company, had a reputation in which they took considerable pride. They had been at one time under the command of a young subaltern whose heroic defence of Hill 60 on May 1, 1915, is on record in the pages of "Eyewitness" and the *Official History of the War*. On that occasion the German army made use of poison gas as a preliminary to attack. A green cloud swept over the trenches, already shattered by a heavy barrage, and killed nearly all the defenders. But the five who remained alive, choking and nearly blinded, fought on under the command of this subaltern, and when the evening came Hill 60 was still ours. This gas attack, observes the *Official History*, " marks a stage in history, as it was the first by which the enemy gained no advantage. . . . The forbidden weapon had been faced and defeated for the first time." The subaltern, whose name was Robin Kestell-Cornish, was now in command of A Company, though, owing to an injury, he was not present at this tour of trenches, and his old platoon was looked on with a kindly eye when old soldiers returned to the regiment. In fact, the platoon was mainly composed of regular soldiers, although at this stage of the war there were few left in the other companies of the regiment. Several of the non-commissioned officers had been continuously with the company since the battle of Mons. So far as I could judge, war being their trade, they regarded the length of it with some indifference. One went so far as to confess to me that he was looking forward to the end of the war, as he wanted to " get back to some real soldiering." My platoon sergeant, on the other hand, was never happy unless he was situated in the most dangerous trenches. He was a kindly, gentle sort of person, who carried on an affectionate correspondence with a large number of young persons in his native London, and had no natural predisposition towards fighting. I was surprised on that account to find him always bright and contented in the most exposed part of the front line, unhappy in the support trenches, and positively morose behind the lines. I commanded No. 1 Platoon for a substantial period, but I remember no occasion when their morale was depressed even by the most trying circumstances. I was therefore amused one night when, passing along the trench line, I overheard a conversation between two old soldiers. " The company is not what it was," one of them said ; " the lads don't go looking for bullets like they used to in the old days."

If the men did not look for bullets, they took no obvious steps to avoid them. Their long experience of fighting stood them in good stead. Every soldier must have remarked how frequently a young soldier was killed in his first few days at the front, while old soldiers, in the words of the song, "never died." The explanation lies, not in the vagaries of a blind fortune, but in the development of an additional sense, which gave warning of the presence of danger. This sense gave the trained soldier a facility for picking out the weaker points in a trench line, and dead ground when in the open; but it gave him also a real prescience which is very difficult to explain. I will give two instances out of many in my knowledge. One night, when it was pitch dark, I was following my company commander, a very experienced soldier, down a communication trench leading directly away from the German lines. Suddenly he fell on his knees; I thought this rather a joke, but I negligently bent over him. A fraction of a second later a rifle grenade burst on the parapet exactly where my head had been. We picked ourselves up, and I said, "I did not see that coming." "No," he replied; "I did not see it, and I did not hear it, but I knew it was there." Some months later, when I had gained that invaluable sense, I happened to be halted with my platoon behind a bank near Thiepval; the bank denied observation from Thiepval Château, but was open to the north, where two miles away across the Ancre the German line ran before Beaumont-Hamel. Suddenly I had a feeling that we had been observed from that direction, and I moved the platoon fifty yards farther on. A moment later four shrapnel shells burst over the exact spot from which we had moved.

Perhaps, therefore, my two old soldiers, their heads high above the parapet in Trench 121 on this winter night, knew by instinct that the machine gun which traversed the parapet all night was set on a line just above their heads at the particular point where they stood on guard. At any rate, the night passed without incident, though the weather was deplorable.

Dawn came at last, and I found behind the craters an unclean and rat-ridden dug-out which was dignified by the title of company headquarters. Behind was waste land, utterly desolate, stretching up to the ridge with the gaunt trees where once had been the Albert—Bapaume Road, now an overgrown grass track, where in the interlocking shell-holes it could be discerned. In front lay the ghastly cemetery with the broken crosses. I was joined by my company commander, and we set out to ascertain whether a way could be found through the medley of blown-in trenches and shell-holes to the regiment on the right of the craters. We had the secondary object of effecting the proper burial of a long-dead Frenchman. We met with no success in either quest. I rested during the morning, so far as was possible in the unhappy circumstance that a sniper had marked the dug-out and devoted the day to shooting into it. The thud, thud of the bullets on the earth was monotonous, but it was a warning against careless movement, and suggested the need of calculating the exact interval between shots with a view to one's safe passage into the trench outside. I spent part of the morning in reading the local trench diary, which gave an account of the more dangerous localities and a variety of comment. I was amused to find some literary contributions by one of my contemporaries at Rugby, who has since become important in the world of letters. Unhappily these contributions had been disfigured by the ill-natured comments of a fire-eating captain of another regiment.

In the afternoon my tour of duty was enlivened by the reported discovery of the position of one of the German trench-mortar batteries. I hurried on to headquarters to report to the colonel. He was delighted. With his adjutant and other headquarters officers and myself he took up a position on a convenient fire-step, and commented excitedly on each puff of smoke emerging from the German trench in the position which I indicated. The row of heads along the parapet, even in the support line, inevitably presented a suitable target, and a moment later a rifle grenade landed with precision in front. The row of heads moved down and up again with all the precision of physical drill on the parade ground. The excitement was intense. I was sent off with orders to clear our front-line trenches of men in order that the heavy artillery might open fire on the far edge of the craters. I fled precipitately down Gowrie Street, but three feet of mud hardly make for great speed. Evening came at last. A shrill and mournful wind swept over the waste. The ground, scarred, pitted, and black with explosive, darkened in the twilight to a uniform grey. The untouched crucifix was black against the evening sky. Gowrie Street, in its mud-ridden desolation and misery, assumed yet more sinister an aspect as I set forth for my first complete night in a front-line trench.

A burst of machine-gun fire traversing the parapet of the front-line trench heralded the approach of night. The light faded out of the sky. I passed along the trench, stopping now and again to speak to a man, or to arrange some piece of work for the night. The moon rose and shed its glare over " No Man's Land," outlining against the sky the stakes and broken lengths of barbed wire and the heads of the men on watch. It passed through my mind that this was Britain's frontier, and that here for mile after mile her chivalry stood on guard in mud and snow, through the long watches of the night, weary but indomitable, surrounded by manifold forms of death, surveying across grim " No Man's Land " an ever-watchful enemy.

The other subaltern in the company, becoming bored, announced his intention of visiting the craters on a reconnaissance, while I, to assist him, undertook to fire Verey lights. These made everything as plain as day as they descended, and revealed a German in one of the craters; unhappily, they first revealed my companion to the German, who got in the first grenade, and indubitably had the best of the encounter. I had left the position which I had taken up for the night in order to fire the lights. While I was returning and was alone in the trench the " nightly strafe " unhappily occurred. It had become the unpleasant practice of the German to select a particularly exposed piece of trench, and to concentrate on it at one time of the night every gun, Minenwerfer, and other instrument of frightfulness available. My first experience of a barrage occurred when I did not expect it, and when

I was alone. I admit that I clung close to the parapet, almost wild with fear, while all round and over the trench shells exploded in such numbers that the crashes and explosions blended in one hideous and prolonged cacophony far louder than thunder, while from end to end the trench was ablaze with a light far more blinding than lightning. A shelter under the parapet looked most uninviting, but I pulled myself together, and passed on to the position which I had selected as my headquarters for the night and had left for the purpose of firing the Verey lights. A heavy shell had scored a direct hit on it. My fortune had evidently been good.

At last, after interminable hours, the ground changed slowly from black to grey: the trenches became more and more distinct ; I could see the colour of the mud, and the haggard whiteness of men's faces. A light breeze swept through the rank grass and desolation of the battlefield, heralding a winter dawn. Round the corner of the trench there was a sound of voices. The trench broke into life. I observed Private Macnab, the only Scotchman in the company, smile. A dixie appeared round the corner of a traverse. The hot tea and rum had arrived.

I picked up my possessions and, after posting the day sentries, slipped away through the mud of Dunfermline Avenue to a deep dug-out at Burnt island, to which company headquarters had been moved. I was soaked through from my thighs downward, and my gum-boots were inches deep in glutinous mud, but I sank happily on to a wire bed and slept. In the afternoon C Company took over our line; I accompanied Noel Blakeway, a young and most gallant subaltern, down Trench 121 to the cemetery amid the crash of Minenwerfer bombs. In the craters I handed over my last post to him and so parted. I next saw him a dark speck on the German wire beyond the craters in the cold light of dawn.

The next thirty-six hours were spent in the support line some 100 yards up the ridge. The dug-outs here were horrible and the defences quite inadequate. In the evening we " stood to " for the hour before darkness, while our parapet was swept by machine-gun fire from Ovillers-La Boisselle, and then settled down for the night. I was not too tired to forget altogether the loud explosions, the inadequacy of our head cover, and the squeaking of the inevitable horde of loathsome rats.

The next morning was quiet enough, the only incident being the arrival of the padre, who combined with his unfailing bonhomie an unnatural curiosity. This led him to stand open-mouthed in an alcove which afforded an excellent view of La Boisselle, but had the further advantage of constituting the local sky-line. The whiplash of a bullet deafened him in one ear, and he resumed his journey at a more reasonable level. In the afternoon a very young subaltern of the Highland Light Infantry, evidently on his first visit to the trenches, passed down Dunfermline Avenue with a carrying party. The usual desultory shelling was in progress. A little while afterwards another party came in the other direction, with stretchers. It was the subaltern and his party returning home, and so they passed westwards on their last journey.

Late that night my company took over another sector of the front line. I had had a little disturbed sleep, and woke feeling sick. I was a moment late, and so missed the head of my platoon. I fitted myself into the slowly moving line of men, and entered a deep and narrow trench known as Kirkcaldy Street. The rattle of rifles and accoutrements against the sides of the trench made so much noise that I felt sure that the Germans could not fail to hear us. Otherwise the night was still. Suddenly there was a blinding flash in the trench just before me; the rush of the air displaced by the shell blended horribly with the roar of the explosion; and a voice cried out in agony, " Christ, my God ! " I am not likely to forget that cry in the night, the blinding flash, and the nauseating smell (afterwards to become so familiar) of blood and explosive which pervaded the whole trench. I escaped with a scratch. There was a mess to be cleared up, and we were jammed like sardines in a narrow trench. It was some time before the relief of the front line was effected.

The rest of the night passed quietly. The trench which we occupied had lately been dug in advance of the old front line, now the support line, by the 18th Division. In consequence it was cleaner than most trenches, and less redolent of decay. Our left flank was, however, exposed; a gap of several hundred yards lay between us and the next regiment, and through the night constant patrolling was necessary. The trench was, moreover, subject to enfilade machine-gun fire from the ruins of Ovillers-La Boisselle, against which a number of overhead traverses provided insufficient protection. The headquarters dug-out had evidently been spotted by the Germans, as it suffered from continuous shell fire. Rifle grenades also were becoming fashionable, and degenerated into a considerable nuisance.

Apart from these discomforts the left sector was very tolerable, and a great contrast to the right sector with its mine craters. On patrol one night with a sergeant I stalked a supposed

German, but nothing came of it. One morning, strangely enough in rather a quiet hour, the cry of a man in agony rose from the German lines. The hour was so quiet that I had time to think, and I found myself feeling a certain pity for him. But it was not long before the uneasy lines broke into wakefulness again, and in the storm of shell fire I had time only for my own affairs and those of my men.

The night of our relief came at last, and I waited in desperate patience for the incoming regiment. The last hour of waiting is always the longest. The trench lines looked like scars in the fitful moonlight, and the chalk of the mine craters gleamed white. Behind us, on the near horizon, stood the shell-torn poplars of the great road, grim sentinels against the background of starry sky.

Over the night, as though from nowhere in particular, a whispering sound came as of a giant's sigh, ineffably eerie, rising into a rolling crescendo and tearing the night air. I crouched against the parapet. Then with four tremendous crashes the great shells exploded in a trench leading back to the ridge by the poplars, and the sky was lit with a glare, as it were, of sheet-lightning.

I straightened myself out, and thought rather bitterly that the Germans might be trusted to know the night of our relief. And then again

came the giant's sigh. Machine guns swept
" No Man's Land " from both sides, and our
field guns opened fire on La Boisselle. For
some time the storm raged, then, as suddenly
as it commenced, died down. In the distance
there was a glare in the sky and the thunder of
far-off guns. The night was likely to be quiet
now, for every gun would be turned towards
the new centre of activity. After all, we were
only pawns in the game.

There was a stir down the trench. The
relief had arrived. We filed down the trench
towards the craters and then westwards towards
the ridge. There were many blocks and vexatious delays. In many places the trenches had
been blown in by the heavy shells, and machine
guns swept the ridge. The shell fire had
caught one of our companies in its process of
relief, and had taken its toll. We passed on,
came to the Bapaume Road, and, forming up,
marched away from all the evil of La Boisselle
down the ghostly road over the Ancre Bridge
and past the White Château. Soon my platoon
was comfortably installed in a house on the
Aveluy Road, and I viewed with unqualified
pleasure a real bed, on which was spread my
sleeping-bag. I crept inside, and, warm, clean,
and dry for the first time for a week which had
seemed like many months, I forgot all the ills
that flesh is heir to in dreamless sleep.

CHAPTER VI

A CITY OF THE DEAD

THE English language is reputed to present special difficulty to students on account of the variety of meanings which a single word may carry, and the constant changes which are always taking place. Terms of endearment become in the course of a few years terms of abuse, and earnest foreigners have been known to cause grave offence by the use of expressions which have the high authority of Shakespeare but have since fallen into desuetude. The process of change in the meaning of words was subject to considerable acceleration during the war. My first week spent in the trenches of La Boisselle may seem in retrospect to have been both noisy and precarious. For the purpose of official records, and in the common parlance of the trenches, it enjoyed the description of " quiet." The succeeding week spent in the town of Albert represented a period of " rest."

The precise significance of this word was borne in on my mind within a short space of time. After a week in the snow-bound trenches of La Boisselle, in the course of which I had had a few hours only of fitful sleep, I had fallen blissfully asleep in my billet in Albert. The hour of the night was late owing to the conditions under which the relief of the front-line trenches had been carried out. Shortly after dawn I became aware of a familiar figure bending over my bed, and when I had been sufficiently awakened I received orders to return at once to the La Boisselle mines on a carrying fatigue. In all the monotony of trench warfare there was no greater tedium than that of the carrying parties which were needed for the supply of material to the front-line trenches, and no greater patience and tact than that of the officers and non-commissioned officers of the Royal Engineers, on whose behalf the carrying parties for the most part worked. The infantry soldier regarded himself as a fighting man and could not be persuaded to take kindly to the rôle of pack animal. Soldiers who could be relied on to remain cheerful in the most exposed trenches in the front line became unwilling and resentful on fatigue. The daily lot of an officer in a field company of the Royal Engineers was to meet a body of over-tired infantry, nominally enjoying a period of rest, but in fact more busily employed than in the line, led by an embittered subaltern. In public the infantry reviled the sappers day and night ;

in private they extended an admiration, no greater than was due, to a body of men who never enjoyed a period of even nominal " rest " out of the line, who endured many of the dangers and discomforts of the infantryman's life, yet were denied the occasional moment of exultation which was his compensation and reward.

The broad *route nationale* leading from Albert to La Boisselle had appeared in the small hours of the morning the friendliest of roads as I emerged on to it from the knee-deep mud of the communication trenches; as I returned at the head of my weary company I felt that I had never seen a road which I so much disliked, and my feelings, which were clearly shared by my men, were not rendered more amicable by the sight of a number of deep shell-holes of unmistakably recent origin. The sapper officer to whom I reported had no doubt learned, as part of his duties, the way to humour tired infantry, and we were at once on excellent terms. This state of affairs was due in part to the regard in which the mining company employed in the La Boisselle mines was held. The one occupation which the infantry admitted to be more hazardous and less enviable than their own was that of the men whose daily lot was to descend the mine shafts in and around the cemetery of La Boisselle. I descended a shaft on one occasion, and although assured by the officer on duty that there was no safer place on the Western Front, I ascended again with remarkable speed, preferring the hazards of an open-air life in the mine-craters to the narrow galleries, driven above and below the German galleries, where men lay always listening to the tap of enemy picks, and waiting for the silence which was ever the prelude to the blowing of mine or counter-mine. The men of my regiment, being drawn from an agricultural community, had a particular dislike for mining fatigues. The miners themselves, for the most part following their traditional occupation, never appeared happy until they reached the mines. Work during the war was not always well distributed. While watching my Dorsets passing in and out of mines, which had for them all the terrors of unfamiliarity, I recollected that some weeks before my company of Durham miners had been employed in cutting brushwood, an occupation which made them laugh so heartily and so long that it was carried on with little success.

The day of rest drew on, and I found myself again at the crucifix on the eastern edge of Albert with visions of resuming my interrupted sleep. The vision faded as my company commander was observed to be coming up the road, and I learned that he had been charged by the brigade commander with the duty of plotting on the map the contour line of visibility from the village of La Boisselle. This occupation presented features of interest to anyone enjoying minor hazards. The routine was simple. We moved forward until we could see the German front line, and in such an interval as the German snipers thought fit to afford took two bearings, one on the tower of Albert Church and one on the spire of Martinsart. A rapid retreat was followed by a brief appearance at another point, until the contour line had been completed.

Life in the town of Albert presented certain amenities not commonly enjoyed by combatant troops. In days of peace it had been a small manufacturing town, destitute of any feature of historic interest, but clearly substantial and prosperous. Deserted now by its inhabitants, but still having many houses but little damaged by shell fire, it afforded billets with real beds, carpets, and armchairs in lieu of the lath-and-plaster barns, sodden camps or rat-ridden dug-outs which were usually allotted to infantry when they were withdrawn from the trench lines for a period in brigade or divisional reserve. The officers' mess for battalion headquarters and the two companies in Albert was in the White Château. I still retain in my mind recollections of this château as a place of singular comfort and admirable design, but I suspect that the surroundings from which I had come, and to which I was so soon to return, conferred on it by force of contrast a beauty which it never had. Perhaps also the White Château is invested in my memory with something of the splendour of those who came there for a few brief hours and passed on to the Somme battlefield, to La Boisselle and Fricourt, and as the summer wore on to Pozières and Contalmaison, and up that long road whose every yard is marked by our dead from the white chalk of the great crater of La Boisselle to the grim slopes of the Butte de Warlencourt. The White Château is gone; not a trace remains. It would not have been fitting that it should stand, in mockery of those who were its lords, though for a brief hour only, and now are dust. Did it stand, the laughter of men on whom the presence of death had no power to cast a shadow could not but linger, echoing in its walls, and the sound of that laughter would break the hearts of men who heard it once but will never hear it again.

The White Château was solidly built, and at this early period of the war not seriously damaged. Its fate was inevitable if heavy fighting commenced, as the trench lines were not far distant. The German gunners rightly surmised that its apparent comfort would inevitably lead to its use as a headquarters, and adopted the practice of sending over a few shells at those hours when it might be expected that a meal was in progress. The approach to the château from my billet at the dinner-hour always presented an interesting mathematical problem, in which the distance between two bits of cover and the interval between two rounds of battery fire formed respectively the known and the speculative elements. The first 100 yards presented occasional shelter where the walls of the houses had not been entirely obliterated; the last 150 yards were devoid of cover. The sudden whoop and roar of battery fire on this open stretch of road made my progress from time to time unusually rapid.

The château attracted the heavier guns. One night as we sat at dinner there was a deafening crash, and the mess became silent for a moment. A major, who was in command at this time, asserted amid general incredulity that one of our own guns was firing. Another, and louder, crash failed to convince him. A captain on the brigade staff had opened a book on the distance of the nearest shell-hole, and was offering, as I thought, unnecessarily short odds on the lowest distances. Another crash and the entry of a large piece of shell by the front door convinced the major at last, and the mess servants were sent down into a cellar. The mess sat on, waiting for further instructions. There was, in fact, little point in moving, as the shells were so heavy that no cover available was likely to be of use.

It was an odd experience. The heaviest shelling in the trench lines was familiar to everyone; but it was strange to be sitting at ease round a table lit by candles, in a comfortable room hung with tapestry, and to expect momentarily the whole to disappear, as suddenly as Cinderella's palace on the stroke of midnight. I saw no outward concern on anyone's face, and for my own part, though a little uncomfortable, I felt singularly detached. I realised that the apprehension of danger is to a great degree dependent on physical conditions. In the darkness and solitude of the trenches, and after many days of continual noise and sleeplessness, the constant mastery of fear is difficult to maintain; in a lighted room in the company of friends, it is easy. Still the odds against a direct hit being scored were very short, and for a moment there was an uncomfortable silence. This was broken appropriately by the padre, who, in a manner devoid of all concern, commenced a story which, to my regret, I feel unable to place on record.

The château was in fact hit, and the room shook. But no one was damaged, and shortly afterwards a merry party was engaged in measuring the distance of an enormous shell hole for the purpose of adjudicating the bets, at the same time calling on their heads the wrath of some neighbouring field-gunners, who asserted that their battery position was being revealed to the Germans by the swinging of my lantern.

Day and night we were shelled. The square by the cathedral was the most dangerous place, and here we lost some good men. Our transport was so repeatedly shelled, and had so many casualties, that it had to move back to Millencourt. Security, however, was not always conferred by moving out of the town, as we discovered in the course of a football match in a neighbouring field. The game was terminated, without definite result, owing to a battery opening fire with shrapnel. This disregard of the decencies on the part of the German Army was the subject of much unfavourable comment. On another occasion our brigade headquarters was hit and the signalling officer killed. My billet was not seriously damaged during my few days there, but on one occasion the noise and clatter of falling masonry were so loud that I supposed that the top story had gone. In fact, it was the house opposite. A man's breeches rose high in the air, and descended into the road, shortly followed by the man himself. He had just taken them off when the shell removed them. The humour of the situation entirely escaped him, and he expressed himself with some freedom, oblivious of the good fortune which had provided that his breeches, and not himself, had been blown through the roof. The night was more disturbed than the day, and often I used to stand at my bedroom window, which looked out on the church, watching the great shells bursting in the square and illuminating in a fitful and unreal light the ruins of this desolate and twilight city.

Indeed, Albert at night after the rising of the moon assumed something almost of beauty, and in thought I can still wander through its ghostly streets. I see the Millencourt—Albert road stretching before me grey amid the darkness of the surrounding countryside, until the line of tall trees marking the *route nationale* looms before me at the western entrance to the town. The road descends under a railway bridge. Below lies Albert in the valley of the Ancre. The cathedral rises shattered but magnificent against the background of moonlit sky. The tower is riven by shell fire. From its summit the image of the Virgin and Child has been torn from its pedestal, but has not yet fallen; the outstretched arms of the Virgin seem to offer the Child to the broken and suffering town beneath. The houses are rent by a thousand scars; yet as the moon sheds its radiance on them it confers something of calm and healing. The town is asleep, as many other cities, but this is a city of the dead.

There is a roar, as of an approaching train coming nearer and nearer. But no train has crossed this bridge for many a day. A moment later a sheet of lurid flame leaps from the cathedral square, and the thunder of the explosion echoes endlessly through the deserted streets. The bridge shakes, and some loose mortar falls.

I pass down a long street; in every ruined house my footfall echoes. Often the cellar and a heap of brick and plaster are all that remains. The moon reveals many strange sights, here the billiard-table piled with rubbish of some estaminet, here an unfinished meal, here a mattress blown through a shattered window. The many human touches to be seen all around increase the sense of desolation. For here is the reverse side of war, the evidences of the sudden flight of a defenceless people into homeless night. The ruined cathedral, battered indeed by innumerable shells, still conveys the impression of majesty, of the victory of eternal faith. But there is no glory in these poor ruined homes. They speak only of the suffering of the inarticulate multitude, of the cruelty of war.

At the corner of the street leading to the church lie the remains of a cycle factory. The roof has disappeared long ago, and a great mass of twisted girders and fallen masonry is piled in inextricable confusion below. Through the gaping holes in the walls the moon reveals thousands of rusted iron frames and gears. A wild cat strangely human in this scene of desolation is outlined on a jagged wall. Near at hand is the railway station. Rank grass grows everywhere, through a hundred crevices on the lifeless platforms and luxuriantly amid the rusted lines. Here, too, where once crowds jostled in changing scenes of animated life, reigns universal death.

I turn towards the cathedral and come to the square. Every house has been utterly destroyed. The very ruins have been swept away. The moon plays strange tricks of fancy through the great rents in the walls of the cathedral, illuminating here a fragment of stained glass, here a broken mosaic, here a Madonna, here the figure of a saint. A soldier stands on guard under the tower, accentuating the desolation of the scene. I cross the square to speak to him, and stand for a moment under the great gilt figure of the Madonna.

A CITY OF THE DEAD

Clouds pace across the sky over the summit, and by a strange illusion the tower appears to be moving and the Madonna to be descending ever lower. There is a whine rising into a scream, and four shells strike the tortured building. There is a clatter of falling masonry, and a cloud of dust rises from the ruins. Then all is quiet again, and the cathedral stands symbolic in ineffable majesty, eternal and serene.

I turn towards the ghostly whiteness of the château and then over a bridge on to the Bapaume road. A challenge rings out and echoes through the shattered houses. Pack-mules loaded with rations and the creaking wagons of a long ammunition column pass by in never-ending procession. The houses become fewer, and at last the great trees of a wayside calvary mark the limit of the town. From a battery position on the slopes leading down to the Ancre the boom of a heavy gun sounds, and a shell passes screeching overhead. A sudden light leaps from a village far in the German lines. Men and horses pass ceaselessly over a rise in front, silhouetted momentarily against the sky. From horizon to horizon innumerable flares rise from the sleepless lines amid the interminable rattle of musketry and the vicious bark of light guns. Behind me lies a city of ghosts and shadows fast bound in the sleep of death.

Our few days of "rest," while in brigade reserve in Albert, came to an end, and I found myself late at night progressing slowly down the long communication trench known as St. Andrew's Avenue towards the cemetery of La Boisselle. The moon had risen and illuminated the sides of the trench, and the faces of men of the outgoing regiment, haggard and worn, as they passed down. The usual blocks occurred from time to time, accompanied sometimes by recriminations and sometimes by the form of boisterous and good-humoured sarcasm which was the *argot* of the trenches. On reaching the battalion headquarters dugouts I found that the direct route, by Dunfermline Avenue, was impassable owing to the heavy shelling and was ordered to make a detour. This formed a pleasant augury for the succeeding week, which did not enjoy the description of " quiet " even in the trench diary. Indeed, the events of the week, as detailed quite truly by the German Daily Wireless, brought the village of La Boisselle, afterwards to become so well known, before the world for the first occasion in its history. A hazardous enterprise was carried out in the vicinity of the village by my regiment with a distinguished valour which led to special mention in Sir Douglas Haig's dispatches, but unhappily met with no success. This enterprise was one of the earliest raids, but the technique of the raid had not at that time been developed, and the form which it assumed, and the forces employed, gave it a greater resemblance to a night attack on a small scale. It is perhaps worthy of description, as the raid, in a rather different form, became a common feature of trench warfare, particularly when the identification of the German regiments in the line was a matter of moment before a battle.

The days preceding the raid were distinguished by shell fire of an intensity which in itself might almost have expunged the word " quiet " from the diary. Coming in one afternoon after taking the morning tour of duty in the mine craters, I found the headquarters dug-out isolated by a rifle-grenade and oil-can barrage. The trench was blown in all round and almost impassable. An old private in the Manchesters, who had come up on fatigue, lay horribly dead across the entrance. There was no " cunningest pattern of excelling nature " here. An officer passing by was blown down the dug-out steps. Our telegraph wires were broken, and the men who attempted to mend them were brought in badly wounded and bathed in blood. At last a breathless orderly came safely through. His arrival was a tribute to his resolution, but a greater tribute to his good fortune. As I took his message,

I thought that it must be of vital importance. It proved to be, in fact, a futile routine message about the proportion of blankets per man in the present state of the weather. A second message was more apposite and the occasion of some mirth. It detailed the times at which burials would take place in the various cemeteries in the neighbourhood.

There was a certain grim humour also in the arrival of the post from England. My orderly brought a letter to me late at night in an exposed corner of the front line. It proved to be a quaintly spelt missive from a very young cousin, full of gossip of home, concluding with the words—" we often talk and think about you and wonder where you are." The question received an immediate answer, as it coincided with the "nightly strafe," and the lurid light from countless explosions along the trench lines made clear the ruins of the village and cemetery of La Boisselle.

We had, however, one quiet night in the sector to the north, fronting Ovillers. These trenches were little shelled, and the contrast with the mine craters was such that I felt a certain exultation. I even found an element of romance in the rat-tat of the machine guns in the stillness of the night, the whoop of bullets passing far overhead, the sigh of the great shells and the glare in the sky as they exploded in

Albert city, the sudden burst of fire from the light guns and the vivid flashes on the Aveluy road which spoke of transport caught in the open, the rising and waning of the moon, the glorious panoply of stars overhead, the gradual coming of dawn over the waste fields. Another night was quiet, perhaps because everyone on both sides was occupied in coping with a snow-storm. Winter in the trenches in bad weather caused many casualties from frost-bite, and a night of intense cold, when the infantry on both sides were standing in freezing water and mud up to the knees, appreciably diminished the gun and rifle fire. This night was so bad that it induced almost a sense of camaraderie with those who, though our enemies, were equally the sport of the weather. Passing down a waterlogged and freezing trench I overheard a Dorset soldier arrive at a great truth. He observed to his neighbour, with all the force of sudden revelation, that " They Jerries over there think they be fighting for a cause." It needed just such another night to teach a man, who was every inch a king, so much wisdom :

> Oh, I have ta'en
> Too little care of this ! Take physic, pomp ;
> Expose thyself to feel what wretches feel,
> That thou mayest shake the superflux to them,
> And show the heavens more just.

It was a pity that *King Lear* was not more widely read in the chancelleries and parliaments of Europe in the days preceding the war.

The night of the raid came towards the end of our tour of trenches. After several days and nights of considerable strain I found myself in command of A Company, as my company commander had been sent by the colonel for a month's rest at the Fourth Army School, after a year's continuous trench warfare from the Menin road to the Frise marshes. Throughout the afternoon experienced soldiers (among whom I was not numbered) could tell that news of our impending attack had reached the German Intelligence, as we were subjected to a harassing fire, and registration by new guns on our support and communication trenches took place. I was in a state of inexperienced optimism, and firmly believed that the Germans were wasting ammunition which they would need during the night. I expected that the mine, whose explosion was to be the signal for our attack, would blow the village of La Boisselle high into the air, and that the survivors, if there were any, would soon be prisoners in our hands. As the hour of attack approached I became less sanguine. The night was still in a degree which no night had been before. The broken posts and wire which marked the boundaries of " No Man's Land " and the white chalk of the mine craters were agleam in the moonlight, and it was so clear that I could discern the ruins and broken tree stumps of the village. Yet no shot was fired while a hundred men crawled through our wire into shell-holes in front. Behind them the trenches were lined with men, for the " stand-to-arms " had been passed down. The deathly silence did not augur well, and as the colonel passed down the line I noticed grave anxiety on his face. Then at last the silence was broken by a machine gun firing from the dim ruins of Ovillers and sweeping our parapets from end to end. Then again there was silence. Two minutes to go. One minute. A thought flickered for a moment in my mind that many now very much alive would within a brief minute be dead. The thought passed. Half a minute. Time. The mine exploded. It seemed to me a very small mine. The earth throbbed. Then again, but for one moment only, there was an unearthly stillness. This was succeeded by a weird sound like rustling leaves for a fraction of a second; then with the noise of a hurricane the shells passed, and the whole outline of the German positions was seared with the appalling lightning and thunder of our artillery. There were a thousand flashes, and a lurid light spread over the battlefield, the light seen only in that most dreadful spectacle, a night bombardment. The thunder of the guns was such that speech was impossible. But there was no time to observe the scene, as in an inferno of flashes and explosions the German counter-barrage broke on our lines.

The intensity of the counter-barrage showed beyond a doubt that the German batteries had been standing to their guns and that every detail of our attack was known. The craters and trenches of La Boisselle were evacuated and full of wire in which those of our men who got through the entanglements were at once caught and impaled. Of Germans there were none to be seen, until their bombers closed in from each side. From end to end of " No Man's Land " a hell of machine-gun fire was raging; the trenches were quite untenable.

The signal to retire was given. But our wounded were everywhere, and time and again the survivors went out to bring them in. It seemed incredible that anything could live in that barrage of gun and rifle fire, with the German bombers in full counter-attack, yet our men would not be denied. Two men refused to leave friends who were dying; by some miracle they survived and brought back a wounded man. A young subaltern stayed behind to help a wounded man out of the German trench and in the act was killed on the wire.

Gradually the fire slackened, and only the

rat-tat of the machine guns and the whine of innumerable bullets disturbed the stillness of the night. I could hear the German transport far behind their lines. I was very tired. For five nights in six I had had no rest. At last the " stand-down " came. Yet there were still two hours to day.

Dawn came at last. The ruins of the village and the surrounding trench lines became distinct, and it was day. On the German wire there were dark specks, among them the dead subaltern and my faithful orderly. Behind me lay a city of the dead, beside me the ravished graves of the dead, before me men, my friends, who yesterday had been so full of life and now lay silent and unheeding in death. Anger and bitterness were in my heart against those who had wrought this destruction, an anger which could find no expression in words. Nor have I occasion now to seek words, for I found them afterwards in Gilbert Murray's translation of *The Trojan Women,* and nothing more true has been written about war :

> How are ye blind,
> Ye treaders down of cities ; ye that cast
> Temples to desolation, and lay waste
> Tombs, the untrodden sanctuaries where lie
> The ancient dead, yourselves so soon to die.

CHAPTER VII

SPRING IN PICARDY

"LA guerre," said the soldier in *Le Tombeau sous l'Arc de Triomphe*—"la guerre a perdu son prestige. Et souviens-toi comme il était puissant. On se la figurait féroce et magnifique, dans sa pourpre brûlante de sang et de feu. Elle imposait, comme un soleil noir. A présent on lui donne son vrai nom : une corvée. La plus lourde, la plus monotone, la plus rebutante des corvées." A more accurate description of the war on the Western Front has not been written. The moments of exultation were few and very far between ; the hours of monotony were interminable. A diary of a long period of service in the trenches would be of no greater interest than a diary of any labourer engaged day by day, indifferent and unimpressed, on the forced labour of mechanical employment. The infantry soldier remembers trench warfare for the most part in terms of the long watches of the night, the slow coming of dawn, the few hours of fitful sleep, the unceasing labour on the construction of new trenches and the maintenance of old trenches continuously destroyed by shell fire and rain, the monotonous coming and going of ration and supply parties for ever jamming in the narrow communication trenches. The patrolling of " No Man's Land " during the darker hours of the night, and the repair of the ever-broken barbed wire under the menace of rifle and machine-gun fire, introduced an element of excitement into the dullest trenches. But there was no excitement in the constant shelling by guns of every calibre and by the heavy Minenwerfer, merely disgust at the appalling noise and the unending apprehension of imminent danger. This again was varied only by the yet greater disgust at the sight of the dead and the dying, and of the sufferings of the wounded, which was of daily occurrence in the quietest, and of hourly occurrence in the worst, sectors of the trench line.

I have described in some detail a short period of trench warfare in the trenches fronting the village of La Boisselle. At that time the various features of trench life, afterwards to become so familiar and monotonous, had all the attractions of novelty. The trench warfare of La Boisselle was typical of trench warfare in any bad sector. I have no desire to impose on others the tedium of that form of warfare by giving my experiences in other trench sectors, where the landscape was the only novelty, and the routine was ever the same. I have selected for description incidents which varied the monotony and made an impression on my mind at the time.

During the winter of 1915–1916 an uneasy calm had brooded over the trench lines on the Somme. No heavy fighting had taken place; the line had remained stable since September 1914, when in the course of the race for the sea the French had established themselves before Amiens and Albert but had failed to drive the Germans from the ridge dominating the valley of the Ancre on the west and commanding a wide view over the country between Bapaume and Cambrai to the east. The incessant local fighting by mine and counter-mine at La Boisselle and Fricourt brought these villages into some prominence; and the town of Albert had achieved a certain fame owing to the statue of the Virgin and Child which lay dependent from the tower of the church and the legend that the war would end on the day on which they fell. Otherwise the Somme battlefield had no history, and was reputed on that account to be happy.

The heavy fighting of 1915 had taken place to the north on the heights of Vimy and Notre Dame de Lorette and round the mining villages of Loos and Hulluch. Here the tide of battle had ebbed and flowed, devastating a wide area of country; on the Somme the trenches of 1914 were still occupied, and within a distance of three miles from the front line it was easy to forget the existence of the war. A reserve line was in process of construction, and occasional shallow trenches were found at the side of the road, where small forces had come into conflict during the time when the tide of the German advance had flowed over Northern France. Otherwise the countryside was not yet disfigured; the villages showed no traces of shell fire; the peasantry carried on their traditional occupations; and the British forces were so small that they were absorbed easily into the villages when they were at rest, and interrupted but little the normal life of the French countryside.

A change was discernible as soon as the Battle of Verdun broke out. The French Army in Artois was relieved by British forces, and the divisions on the Somme were no longer isolated from the rest of the British Army. The line became continuous from the canal bank north of Ypres to the village of Frise on the Somme. New divisions arrived; new railways and roads were constructed; new gun-pits were everywhere to be found; dumps of material grew larger day by day. The villages became inconveniently overcrowded. It was soon evident that the long period of inactivity was at an end, and that the Somme battlefield was to be the scene of the great offensive of 1916. The first news reached us early in April. At this time the 32nd Division was holding the line from Thiepval Wood to La Boisselle. Our line was now shortened so that it extended only to Authuille Wood. Old soldiers were well aware that the line held by any body of combatant troops is reduced for one reason only—the imminence of an attack. The news gave every satisfaction. The morale of the regiment was high. The continual hardships and heavy casualties sustained by the regiment in the trench warfare of the preceding winter had been such as to make the prospect of an attack alluring. Of the success of the offensive few of us had the smallest doubt. We had at last the men and the guns. Confidence reigned supreme; none of us expected to spend another winter in France, and an announcement by the quartermaster that he had been asked to report on the form of winter clothing which had proved of most value in the last winter with a view to its adoption in the coming winter was regarded as an unnecessary exhibition of fussiness on the part of the authorities. Not yet had the British Army learned to greet the changes and chances of a war of attrition with the proverb " The first ten years will be the worst."

The battle order was soon disclosed. The 34th Division, composed for the most part of Northumberland Fusilier battalions from Tyneside, came into the line at La Boisselle. Our old trenches fronting Ovillers were occupied by the 8th Division, a regular division with a great reputation. Within our area of attack lay the Leipzig Redoubt and the village of Thiepval. This might be regarded as a compliment to the division, as Thiepval, being a key position and dominating the valley of the Ancre, had been fortified by the Germans with the utmost ingenuity and resource. The vital importance of the position had been early recognised, and a regiment had been placed there as its permanent garrison, never to be relieved. This regiment had constructed a labyrinth of underground passages, leading from the deep cellars of the village in all directions. Under bombardment the troops were withdrawn into these cellars; the moment the bombardment lifted they manned again their machine-gun emplacements, and met attacking troops with a concentration of fire through which no man could pass unscathed. Such was the strength of the fortifications, that even the massed artilleries of the Somme could not obliterate them. On the morning of the attack sixteen shells a second were exploding in the village; yet the attacking division was practically wiped out by machine-gun fire. The Germans rightly held that their fortress was impregnable to frontal attack ; it fell ultimately when the advance in the south had made possible attack from the flank and rear.

On taking over the trenches fronting Thiepval we found the 36th (Ulster) Division astride the Ancre. Their trenches were in splendid order, and everyone was impressed by the resolute and disciplined bearing of the Ulster regiments. North of the Ancre was the 4th, a Regular division, which old soldiers remembered in the later stages of the retreat from Mons. Beyond them and to the north of Beaumont-Hamel was the 29th Division, lately arrived from Gallipoli. We were interested to meet the division which had made history on the beaches of Cape Helles a year before. The Germans greeted their arrival, and adequately expressed their sense of the occasion, by a night bombardment of great intensity followed by a raid. I remember the occasion well for several reasons. I had just carried out the relief of the front line near Thiepval Château, and was proceeding down the trench towards my headquarters dug-out to have dinner, when without any warning the barrage descended on the trenches beyond the Ancre. For a moment I hesitated ; then the fury of the gun fire showed that there was to be no dinner as yet. Having expressed my disgust in a suitable manner, I gave the order to stand to arms. Then I turned to watch with interest the tremendous artillery battle. Heavy guns were firing from far in the south, and the sky was ablaze as far as the eye could reach. The boom of the guns, the screech of the shells passing far overhead, the devastating roar of the explosions, the fountains of black earth thrown skywards, contributed to the eerie grandeur of this terrible scene.

We were not ourselves under very heavy fire, and I thought of the men in the trenches beyond the Ancre crouching under their crumbling parapets and waiting for the savage mêlée of bomb and bayonet which would ensue when the barrage lifted. But only for a moment had I time to think, as there was a series of crashes in the trench, and it became clear that one of our batteries, in retaliating, had mistaken our trench for the German line, and we were being shelled from both front and rear. There was a curtain of fire which cut me off from my headquarters, and I was compelled to make a rather hazardous journey to another company far to the south. I demanded that our artillery should lengthen their range, but received less than no encouragement. The good-natured sarcasm of the gunners was, however, lost on me, and I had the satisfaction of the last word, as they were so tactless as to drop a dud shell into the trench. This I picked up, and, having noted the markings, sent back an orderly with a description of them and other ill-natured comment. In the meantime we were losing men, and the familiar cry of " stretcher-bearer " passed down the trench. I hurried back, and had just found my sergeant-major, where he stood intently watching the German trenches, when there was an overwhelming crash. The sky became a maelstrom of colliding stars, and then turned gold. I seemed to be sailing through space into the most glorious of sunsets, and the world was very far away. I could not struggle, nor did I want to. I had rather a feeling of peace, of relief that the bitterness of death was past. Then the vision began to fade. I became conscious of the surrounding mud and of a familiar face. I felt very sick.

The Thiepval trenches which we held through the spring of 1916 differed greatly from those of La Boisselle. They ran through the garden of Thiepval Château, and in the absence of shell fire there was much that was attractive in the view over the valley of the Ancre and the woods of Thiepval, Aveluy, and Authuille on each side, now beautiful in the glory of spring. Flowers were often to be found growing in the sides of the trenches and in " No Man's Land," and just below my dug-out there were the remains of two red-brick gate-posts which had led from the château garden to the orchard in the valley below. The flowers found their way into dug-outs; the orchard was swept by machine guns night and day, and if the apple trees bore any fruit in 1916 there was no one so foolhardy as to seek it. I was sitting one morning in my dug-out overlooking the orchard when I witnessed a strange little comedy. I was growing drowsy; we had been through a time of great strain. Our trenches had been destroyed by a barrage of great intensity; the Germans had attacked, and there had been heavy fighting with bomb and bayonet in our lines. Now there was a lull. The sun was warm, and a breeze whispered in the shell-riven trees. There was no sound of war but the intermittent thud of a sniper's bullet from the ruins of the château as it struck the earth. I was nearly asleep when my eye was caught by a most unwarlike scene in the entrance to the dug-out. A dud shell lay partly embedded in the dry mud. A mouse with his head on one side peered at me, then took refuge behind the shell, reappearing a moment later on the far side. This was repeated several times. Then, emboldened, the mouse departed and brought back a friend. A game ensued, and whenever I blinked the two mice fell over each other in a ludicrously human way as they sought the security of their strange haven.

The garden of the Thiepval Château was a shell trap of the worst description and our losses here were very heavy, more especially in the days immediately preceding the opening of the Battle of the Somme. The right sector fronting the Leipzig Redoubt was comparatively quiet, but the château trenches, the Broomielaw, the Trongate, Sauchiehall Street, and the Hammerhead and Maison Grise saps were trenches of evil omen. One of these saps ran far into " No Man's Land," and those who ventured to its far end enjoyed the privilege of listening to the conversation of the Germans in an outlying post. A more popular diversion was mispronouncing the names of the trenches for the benefit of three Highland regiments in the division. I remember well a Highland major who on a visit to my dug-out refused for nearly an hour to touch our whisky on the ground that he never drank spirits before noon. I then observed casually that he had presumably come through " Saucy Hall " Street on his way up the line. The effect was instantaneous, and much of the bottle had gone before he was sufficiently revived.

The German trench mortars had been responsible for many casualties at La Boisselle ; here they cost us a heavy toll of life. Men were blown to pieces and buried, and the noise of the explosions was so appalling and continuous as to cause an almost intolerable strain. If our guns opened fire, the Germans did not attempt to silence them by a counter-battery demonstration, but put down a Minenwerfer barrage on the infantry; and it caused us particular annoyance that the activities of the Ulster Division trench mortars invariably provoked retaliation on our, and not their, trenches. The excellence of our own trench mortars was some consolation to us. The officer in charge of them was a redoubtable Irishman, very keen on his job and fearless to a fault. One of his assistants, also an Irishman, wasted my time one night in a prolonged attempt to persuade me to let him go on a visit to the German trenches. He asserted that no man could reasonably be expected to lob a trench mortar bomb into a trench unless he had first had a look into it to see where the bomb would fall.

Behind the château trenches lay Johnstone's Post, our battalion headquarters, looking out over a wide valley, shell-ploughed and for ever swept by flying bullets, and the great mass of Thiepval Wood dominating the desolate marshes of the Ancre. The wood was never silent, for shell and rifle fire echoed endlessly through the trees, in testimony of the unceasing vigil of the opposing lines. At night the flares, as they rose and fell, threw the wood into deeper shadow and made it yet more dark and menacing. On the edge of the wood a communication trench, Paisley Avenue, a constant mark for the German artillery, led to the high bank above the Ancre. On our side of the valley a better trench, Hamilton Avenue, led also to the bank. On emerging from either of the trenches we had the alternative of proceeding along the main road to Authuille North Barricade or of following a safer track under the bank and on the edge of the stream to a ruined mill on the lower edge of the village. Here was a bridge just wide enough to permit of the passage of a trolley. Beyond the ruins of the village, in which wise men did not linger long, was another high bank, honeycombed by dug-outs, and a long causeway across the marshes known as Blackhorse Bridge.

On the edge of the bank, and just beyond the South Barricade of Authuille village, lay the French cemetery where the dead of the first few months of the war lay beside the dead of centuries of peace. The small cemetery had proved inadequate within a short time, and the graves lay outside and around it. Now there was a new and already large cemetery below. One evening I stood there looking over the broad marshes of the Ancre and the great mass of Aveluy Wood beyond. There

SPRING IN PICARDY

was a lull in the firing, and everything was still. The sun was setting; perhaps the majesty of Nature had stayed for one moment the hand of the Angel of Death. The river and marshes were a sea of gold, and the trees of the wood were tinged with fire. To the south were the square tower of Aveluy Church and the great trees surrounding the crucifix at the junction of the roads, known as Crucifix Corner. Shadows were lengthening in the woods and on the marshes. A cool evening breeze blew gently through the graves of our dead.

Before me lay men of many nations in their long sleep. The names inscribed on the dark crosses of the French were full of music; they were men of the Breton Corps, sons of Morbihan and Finisterre. Apart lay the grave of a man killed in the first month of the war, when Uhlan patrols came into conflict with small bodies of British and French detached from their regiments. Near by were the dead of the first autumn slain in the great fight for the ridge. Beyond were the men who had died in the long and monotonous days of trench warfare, which for eighteen months had taken, day by day, its toll of human life, of the flower of two nations. Here were the white crosses of the British, men from every shire in England and Scotland. Officers and men lay side by side as they fell. The tall Celtic cross of a Highlander was surmounted by his glengarry. The grave of an English officer was inscribed with the words " So long ! " I wondered whether these were the last words of the dead officer, or words written there by one of his comrades who expected soon to see him again. A little way apart were the graves of the Indians, with inscriptions in a strange language, men who died on these bleak uplands so far from their homes, in faithful discharge of a soldier's trust.

In the far corner a padre stood reading the burial service, while a group of men with bowed and uncovered heads stood round a new grave. Here indeed death held nothing of indignity, and all was simple and sincere. It was a scene of quiet grandeur. No king could dream of a more splendid resting-place, here above the marshes in the glory of the evening.

The sun set; twilight drew on. The evening star glimmered above the far horizon. The marshes were grey, and a mist rose from the water. Dark shadows enveloped the woods. There was a roar as a shrapnel shell burst, and the smoke hung like a pall over the ground where once Authuille had stood, now a ruin where death stalked night and day. A machine gun opened fire in the trenches, and the crash of bombs re-echoed through the trees. The weary night watches had begun. The wind rose. The Angel of Death was abroad, and in the wind I could hear the beating of his wings.

Here above the Ancre lie many of the most gallant of my regiment, men who were my friends, men whose memory I shall revere to the end of time. Some of them were soldiers by profession; others had turned aside from their chosen avocations in obedience to a call which might not be denied. Unfaltering and unrepining they offered their lawful heritage of full and splendid life, and trod the dark highway of death without dismay. They have passed into the silence. We hear their voices no more. Yet it must be that somewhere the music of those voices lingers, and that in time to come it will inspire and strengthen men who in pursuit of an ideal may be called upon to make a like sacrifice. But we who have lost our friends know well that much of the richness and beauty of life passed with them for ever from our lives. If we have any consolation, it is that they held their heads high in life, and that when the darkness closed round them they did not flinch.

How well I can recall the line of merry faces in the glare of candles in the mess! Chief among them I see my friend Robin Kestell Cornish. In his presence I had always a sense that it was morning; I could not imagine him growing old. Never have I met anyone so full of the joy of life, yet so careless to preserve it. Eager always for battle, he was magnificent in attack ; in the most trying periods of trench warfare, under continuous shell fire and in every circumstance of hardship, he remained undaunted, resolute, and unfailingly cheerful. He had the rare power of inspiring courage by his presence. Time and again, when passing with him down a line in hours of stress, I have seen the amazing power which he could wield over men who held him in sincere affection and absolute trust. I have met many brave men, but none braver than he. And his courage proceeded, not from recklessness or a failure to appreciate the probable consequences of his actions, but from self-discipline. The first occasion on which this was revealed to me was in a heavy bombardment at La Boisselle. I had come in to the headquarters dug-out from my tour of duty. Another subaltern had gone out. The shelling which had been intermittent became suddenly more heavy. Kestell Cornish rose to his feet. I could see that he was debating whether the highest standard of duty required him to join his subaltern and the sentries in the most dangerous posts, and that he was mastering himself by conscious effort. I asked him whether he regarded it as necessary to attempt to reach the mine craters, as it seemed impossible to get through the curtain of fire. He did not reply, but slowly drew on his equipment and passed out into the trench. Later before Thiepval Château, just before the opening of the Battle of the Somme, an order came through that an advanced trench was to be dug " at any cost." We looked at each other, knowing well what the cost would be. The moon was almost full; the nights were practically cloudless. I remarked that this meant the end of things for most of us. He shrugged his shoulders, and replied that it would be far better to lose one's life than to be put to the necessity of reporting that the trench had not been dug. In the event, as darkness closed and before the moon rose, the company crept man by man into " No Man's Land." Three machine guns were turned on the first man, yet somehow the men were disposed along the line which the trench was to follow. There they lay digging with their hands and entrenching tools in a desperate effort to gain even a few inches of cover before the moon rose. The German machine guns swept up and down the line, and rifle grenades came over unceasingly. Through the summer night Kestell Cornish walked up and down the line, disdaining to take cover, encouraging his men to ever greater efforts, succouring the wounded, staying at the side of the dying. But for the force of his example, the trench could not have been dug. By some miracle he was not hit. On Hill 60 a year before he had won the Military Cross; he won it again that night and on the Ancre in November. On that occasion fighting took place in the most deplorable conditions of weather, and in the course of the battle he contracted frost-bite. He refused to leave the line of shell-holes which was our front line until they were made secure. Unable to stand, he was at last removed on a stretcher. As he was being carried to the rear the Germans counter-attacked, and Kestell Cornish gave the order to his stretcher-bearers to take him back to the line. For three years of constant fighting he escaped death or serious wounds, although courting them always. But it could not be that such courage should not meet at last its reward. In the desolate wastes of the salient he fell wounded by the side of his general, and died in June 1918 at Wimereux. He wrote me a letter a few days before he died. For months he had been in dreadful pains. Now he was dying, but there was no word of complaint on his lips; and that ardour of spirit which had given him the power to sway the hearts of men, and to inspire in them something of his own courage, was never more splendid than in the hour of his passing to that high fellowship beyond our ken.

A man very different from Kestell Cornish, but gifted with the same power to inspire affection in the men whom he led, was W. B. Algeo, the commander of B Company. An "Old Contemptible," he had distinguished himself greatly in the German attack at Ypres early in 1915. On this occasion he was blinded by gas and taken to hospital, but on partially recovering his sight he contrived to escape and rejoined his regiment in the line. He gave the impression of greatly deprecating the war on account of its minor discomforts and its interference with settled habits and regular meals. Its inherent dangers were not judged by him to be worthy of comment. After eighteen months of service in the front line he received the offer of a staff appointment. The message came to him one evening in May when a relief of the line before Thiepval was about to take place. He stood looking over the valley of the Ancre and the woods beyond where the glory of life was instinct in the emerald green of the tall trees. In his hand was a scrap of paper offering him the chance of life and the opportunity of high distinction in his profession. He debated for a little while, and then, turning to one of his subalterns, said, "I can't leave these old men." He went up the line, and within a few hours lost his life in a hazardous enterprise in the garden of Thiepval Château.

Although dawn was breaking, one of the old men whom he had refused to leave went out on his own initiative in a gallant but forlorn attempt at rescue and, refusing to leave him, fell by his side.

Many others of the Dorset Regiment died before Thiepval in the months preceding the battle and on the fateful morning of July 1. Some who were wounded on that morning returned to the regiment and died in later battles of the war. Those few of us who are left may perhaps be pardoned if we have at times the sense of being stragglers.

In a scene to my mind at once the most tragic and the most beautiful in the dramatic literature of our time—in *Le Tombeau sous l'Arc de Triomphe*—the soldier, on whom the dark night of death is already descending, calls his dead friends to be present at his marriage. They only are invited to the most pure of marriages, consecrated between himself and his bride in the stillness and beauty of a summer's night. He raises his glass to salute and to thank them, and when they answer, he replies in lines of splendid eloquence that he does not know whether it is a cup or a chalice which he holds before him.

To those who served in the war this passage has—and clearly had on the night when first I heard it spoken in a silence so tense as to be almost painful—a special beauty and significance. The soldier has not forgotten the dead. The splendid fellowship which we shared has been for most of us the greatest thing in our lives. If we have any pride, it is that once we were accounted worthy of that fellowship. We remember that in the company of men high-hearted and generous we too could live a life of courage and fidelity and could go to death as to a holiday. As the years pass by, and the dust of the arena sullies our ideals, and the petty ambitions and jealousies of an ignoble civilisation absorb our strength and misdirect our endeavour, we can look back almost with longing on days which, however tragic, at least gave us the honour and dignity of being men. We may perhaps realise how rare is the privilege of dying well, and feel a trace of envy at the thought of those who will never grow old, whom " age shall not weary nor the years contemn."

The soldier could not say whether it was a cup or a chalice which he raised to his lips. Who is to say? Those who live, as perforce we were compelled to live, exposed to sun, rain, and wind, surrounded by natural forces, in the constant presence of death, are conscious of a mystery in the heart of things, some identity of man with that which gave him birth, nourishes him, and in due time receives him again. In the life of cities man is protected from the play of natural forces; and death, when it comes, has a suggestion of the unnatural by virtue of its unfamiliarity. But those whose daily lot it is to witness the processes of Nature, the awakening and renewing of life in the miracle of dawn, the coming of rest and sleep in the glory of the setting sun, have a greater opportunity of seeing life and death in their true perspective, a fuller appreciation of the place of man in Nature. Many of the war poets expressed their consciousness of this affinity, their sense of forming part of the Whole, and the contentment which that sense could bring in the presence of death. Most splendid perhaps was *Into Battle*, and those magic lines in which Julian Grenfell had greeted the spring of the first year of the war were often in my mind as we marched on the roads behind the lines between the villages to which from time to time we were withdrawn to rest, Millencourt and Senlis, Bouzincourt and Martinsart, Pierregot and Montigny, happy village of great woods and many châteaux. I watched the coming of spring in the woods, and the young corn in the fields, and the men, the flower of every shire in Britain, on the march towards the chalk uplands of the battlefield. I wondered often how many of those whose eyes were delighted by the glory of these fields would see the harvest, and I thought of that other harvest which Death would reap. Yet, though I knew that the blood of men who were my friends must soon incarnadine these fields, I had in my heart a sense that through their sacrifice life would become more noble in due time. I had not, and I have not, the power to express that which was in my heart. But another man, Allen Seager, saw the spring of 1916 on the Somme, and, conscious that he was at last to meet his long-sought rendezvous with death, wrote his epitaph, and that of the men who were his comrades in that great adventure, in the splendid Lafayette ode :

There, holding still in frozen steadfastness
Their bayonets toward the beckoning frontiers,
They lie, our comrades, lie among their peers,
Clad in the glory of fallen warriors,
Grim clusters under thorny trellises,
Dry furthest foam upon disastrous shores,
Leaves that made last year beautiful, still strewn
Even as they fell, unchanged, beneath the changing moon ;
And earth in her divine indifference
Rolls on, and many paltry things and mean
Prate to be heard and caper to be seen,
But they are silent, calm ; their eloquence
Is that incomparable attitude ;
No human presences their witness are,
But summer clouds and sunset crimson hued
And showers and night winds and the northern star,
Nay, even our salutations seem profane,
Opposed to their Elysian quietude.

CHAPTER VIII

FIGHTING ON THE ANCRE

AMONG the earliest honours borne on the colours of the Dorset Regiment is that of Plassey. The part which they played in that battle is commemorated in their proud title *Primus in Indis* and in a splendid tribute by Macaulay in his Essay on Clive. Among the latest honours of the regiment is a small village on the River Ancre, by name Thiepval. This honour was bought at a far greater price, yet the name has already become unfamiliar except to those who fought in the grim ruins of the village and the fields and orchards surrounding them. These two battles illustrate in some measure the difference between the old warfare and the new, and the later battle must be held partly responsible for the loss of prestige which war, once so magnificent, so dramatic, so effective a means of settling difficult issues, has suffered in the minds of men.

The Battle of Plassey, as described in the majestic prose of Macaulay, has a high dramatic value. We see Clive's dauntless spirit, for the first and for the last time, shrinking from the responsibility of taking a decision; his hours of weakness; his final determination to put everything to the hazard; the battle array of Surajah Dowlah—40,000 infantry, 15,000 cavalry, 50 pieces of ordnance with their white oxen and elephants; the attenuated line of the British forces, 3,000 strong, the men of the 39th Regiment conspicuous among them; the onset of disciplined valour on a confused and dispirited multitude; the victory by which, with " a loss of 22 soldiers killed and 50 wounded, the genius of one man subdued an empire larger and more populous than Great Britain."

In the Battle of Thiepval the disciplined valour of the 39th Regiment was not less conspicuous, yet even the magic art of Macaulay could hardly give it a dramatic value. The Battle of Plassey lasted a few hours, and a full description of it occupies one of Macaulay's shorter paragraphs. The Battle of Thiepval may be said to have begun in April, when my regiment first came into the line fronting the village and engaged in the minor hostilities and the digging and carrying fatigues which were the costly prelude to the attack, and to have ended on July 14, when the regiment was at last withdrawn. During that time there was constant fighting, most conspicuously on July 1, when the British Army advanced to the assault on a front extending from Gommecourt to the Somme. But there was little that was dramatic in the assault of the divisions astride the Ancre. The fortress villages of Serre, Beaumont-Hamel, Thiepval, and Ovillers were impregnable to frontal attack; their machine guns mowed down the attacking infantry as with a scythe. The Dorset Regiment, moving forward from the banks of the Ancre in support of the Highlanders assaulting Leipzig Redoubt, came under the fire of massed machine guns before ever they reached our own front line at the edge of Authuille Wood. A small part of the German front line was captured and held by the few survivors of two Highland regiments, the Border Regiment, and the Dorsets, but this represented the furthest limit of the advance. The splendid exhilaration which accompanies the forward sweep of successful advance over open country after months of trench warfare underground was not the lot of the attacking divisions on the first day of the Somme. The lot of many, if not most, regiments was similar to that of the Dorset Regiment, massacred by the fire of machine guns in Authuille Wood before ever the advance was begun. Dramatic value can hardly be found in the annihilation of the flower of an English county by a death which came whining and screaming through the trees, dealt by an enemy whom no one could see.

But July 1 was one day only in the three months during which the regiment served before Thiepval, and there were many days and nights of fighting more costly than the Battle of Plassey during that time. A detailed record of those months would be intolerable in the constant reiteration of attack and counterattack, day and night bombardment, and unceasing labour, with the dead and wounded passing ever across the foreground, sometimes in a trickle, sometimes in a flood. In the memories of those who took part one day is confused with another, and but a few incidents remain clear, incidents often of a purely personal significance and of no import to the military historian. I have set these down as they come to my memory and in no order of time or place.

I see a sunlit village, with a long street thronged by men of many regiments. It was the late afternoon, and the Dorset Regiment was on parade. The familiar orders were given, and, headed by the drums and fifes, the regiment marched out of the village towards the east and swung along the country roads. All round were the visible signs of impending battle. The roads were thronged with transport which delayed us. We passed through the battery lines of our massed artillery; behind convenient ridges the guns were almost wheel to wheel. The chalk pits, so common a feature of these uplands, were crowded with picketed horses. Evening came, and the broad fields of Picardy, now almost ripe for harvest, were emblazoned by the setting sun with an unforgettable splendour. The evening was in harmony with the thoughts of many of us, for whom this could not but be the last march. Twilight drew on, and when we halted behind a rise on the new road from Bouzincourt to Martinsart it was night. The trees which marked the summit of the ridge to the east were silhouetted against the sky by the light of the flashes from many guns and the flickering star-shells which rose high above " No Man's Land " from the uneasy lines. The march of my regiment towards a battle which all expected to be the greatest in history filled my mind with a certain exultation, dispelling for the time any doubt or thought of fear.

But soon we became immersed in the interminable and vexatious delays which commonly prevail in times of stress when troops and supplies for several miles of trenches have to pass over a bridge subject to shell fire, and a causeway across marshes fit only for pedestrian and mule traffic and subject to constant flooding. When a battle is pending the confusion may be serious, as the noise of transport on a still night is audible many miles away, and an active enemy will maintain a harassing fire on cross-roads, bridges, and other places which are likely to be thickly populated. My platoon was the last of the regiment, and derived the full benefit of all the blocks in the traffic. Our transport, making, as it seemed to me, a din which could not fail to be heard by every gunner in the German army, caught us up, and I expressed to the transport officer my sincere hope that the retribution which the hideous noise made by his wagons richly deserved would fall on the real criminals and not on my innocent platoon.

We moved slowly on through a wooded valley, lined on each side by little streets of illuminated canvas huts in which a pioneer battalion was quartered. The row of dim lights in the darkness of the surrounding trees conferred something of beauty on the scene, and spoke of that rest and freedom from care which we were leaving farther behind us with every stride. We crossed the line of the old narrow-gauge railway and came to the barricade outside Aveluy. We answered a challenge by a sentry who stood on guard in its shadow, then turned to the north and passed through ghostly and barren country into the gloom of Aveluy Wood. Below and to the east was the main railway line from Arras to Paris, which here ran through a cutting: no train had passed this way since 1914, and the lines were overgrown with weeds. A bridge led over the cutting to the marshes of the Ancre, but the bridge and the narrow approaches to it were choked by a jumble of every sort of transport, and so densely packed with men that movement in any direction was impossible. In the tumult of rumour and recrimination which came from the struggling and impenetrable mass one sure fact at length emerged. The causeway across the marshes, known as Blackhorse Bridge, was broken, and the ingoing and outgoing reliefs of two divisions, with their transport, were presenting to the German artillery and machine guns the finest of targets if the chance glare of a bursting shell should reveal their present plight.

Such reflections offered little comfort as we stood above the bridge unable to move forward or backward. A machine gun opened fire on the far side of the marshes. At last there was some sign of movement; an order was passed back that every man was to wade the marshes as best he could. In a little while I found myself surrounded by men invisible below their waists, seeking with indifferent success to keep their feet in the marsh. At length after an eventful struggle I reached the far bank, and, having made a few remarks on the advantages of entering the line in a thoroughly soaked condition, I fell quietly asleep in a neighbouring dug-out, to wake some hours later dry and well content.

From Blackhorse Bridge the way to the south lay along the bank of the river towards Aveluy. Passing this way I found a battery in action in a green meadow leading down to the Ancre. I felt a certain envy of the gunners; they looked so clean and free from care, and they lived in quarters so much better than those of the infantry. Across the river was a small château reputed to have been a shooting-box in happier days. Shooting on the Ancre had of late assumed a different character, and the duck enjoyed a happy immunity, broken only by the occasional depredations of the more leisured gunners. Crucifix Corner lay ahead girdled by tall trees, but I turned aside to enter Authuille Wood. Not yet had the gun fire seriously thinned the trees nor deprived them of their foliage, and the wood was cool and green, in welcome contrast to the sweltering fields and roads, deep in chalk dust, which represented the usual scenery of this countryside. Cool and green on that day were no doubt also those other woods of Mametz, Trônes and Delville, and High Wood, where within a month the horror of modern warfare was to reach its dreadful climax. The wood of Authuille held its presage of things to be, for it was thronged with fatigue parties busily engaged on completing bridges, gun positions, and ammunition dumps. On the eastern edge I came to our front line. Concealed emplacements held guns which were destined to fire over open sights at Leipzig Redoubt when the time came. For the present they were silent.

I came to a bridge over a defile which our plan of attack required us to cross, and examined it with interest. Its span was less than ten yards. A few days later the bridge, marked with unerring accuracy by the German machine-gunners, was heaped with our dead and wounded so as to be almost impassable; and a platoon forty-eight strong on one side emerged with a strength of twelve. But on this summer afternoon I could cross it without apprehension, and from a convenient machine-gun emplacement could survey the Leipzig Redoubt and the long valley up which our advance was planned to sweep. At its far end I saw Mouquet Farm, our objective, the roof sparkling in the sunlight, to all appearance unfortified and at peace. Not for one moment did the thought cross my mind that this wood and the open stretch of " No Man's Land " before me would be carpeted with our dead and wounded, and the trench line less than a quarter of a mile away be the farthest limit of our advance.

My reconnaissance completed, I moved away from the emplacements and into the wood; a moment later the rush and roar of shells resounded through the trees. The German gunners were alert, but the trees gave concealment, and I was able to stroll quietly down an old drive and to enjoy the lights and shadows of this sunlit wood.

I crossed again the shell-scarred meadow bordering the Ancre and turned aside to the gunners whose lot I had envied as I went up the line. I had no occasion to envy it now. The gun emplacement was a shambles; the gun would never fire again.

It was the late afternoon. The officers of the regiment were assembled in a dug-out looking out over the Ancre at Blackhorse Bridge. Plans for the attack were gone over in detail by the adjutant; duties were allotted. Everything was businesslike and matter-of-fact. I have known orders for a field day in England to be given in a more portentous manner. The proceedings were marked by no high seriousness, and occasionally degenerated into hilarity when a duty of unusual difficulty or danger was allotted. This reached its climax when a young officer received instructions that his duty was to convey a

Bangalore torpedo up to and beyond Mouquet Farm, to place it under the wire of the German third line, and, having exploded it, to consolidate beyond this somewhat advanced position. Even our high hopes on the eve of battle did not enable us to visualise quite so remarkable a feat of arms, and no one was more amused than the young officer who had been honoured by this duty. Four subalterns were allotted a duty to them more distasteful, to remain in regimental reserve. One of them, confused and distressed beyond measure by this unexpected blow, raised his voice in protest. The adjutant, ignoring a breach of discipline caused by such great provocation, hurriedly passed on to the next order. The subaltern sat unheeding and inconsolable, with bowed head.

In the best account so far written of the blocking of Zeebrugge the author of *By Sea and Land* describes how he came to take part in an engagement described as " something very pink," and how, as he left the Admiralty and walked round St. James's Park, his heart was in his boots. He then left for Chatham, inspected *Vindictive*, and found in the company assembled there " an atmosphere inimical to anxiety." That happy phrase most adequately expresses the morale of the Dorset Regiment, and indeed of the British Army,

FIGHTING ON THE ANCRE

in June of 1916; and while it is well that we should remember the material horror and carnage of the Somme, it is not well that we should forget that many men there found their manhood, there first knew the triumph of the spirit over fear and fatigue, there enjoyed a comradeship which was in itself a sufficient recompense for all things forfeited.

The dug-outs sheltering under the high bank of the Ancre at Blackhorse Bridge were the headquarters of the battalion acting as brigade reserve in the sector from Thiepval to Authuille Wood. I have therefore many memories of days and nights spent under this high bank, looking out over the broad marshes of the Ancre and the great trees of the wood beyond. Here we constantly paraded in preparation for the relief of trenches and for the incessant fatigues which, as the day of battle drew nearer, became onerous in the extreme. Under the bank the regiment paraded on the fateful morning of July 1, when the thunder of our barrage was such that orders could not be heard. On that occasion the regiment moved to the south to Authuille Wood, but generally our route was to the north through the village of Authuille and up the communication trenches leading to Thiepval.

I remember many summer evenings when, after watching the sun set over the marshes, tingeing them with fire and shedding on all Nature the gift of rest and peace, I turned to the north up the path to Thiepval, where through the night the star-shells rose and fell and the sound of gun and rifle fire echoing without end through the trees spoke of the unresting vigilance of warring men.

One night remains vividly in my mind, though it was without incident and similar to many others. I was detailed for a fatigue, but the shell fire was so heavy that I had some hope that it might be cancelled. The arrangements were, however, in the hands of a subaltern of the Royal Engineers, who, obedient to the traditions of his corps, regarded shell fire as a thing which might exist, but of which he had no official knowledge. We accordingly set out, and as we happened to have only a sergeant with us, we neglected the communication trenches and made across open ground for a spinney which lay near our destination. The moon had risen, and the spinney stood out dark against the moonlit sky, with the great mass of Thiepval Wood rising in dark and menacing gloom beyond, except when a heavy shell bursting on Gordon Castle, in the centre of the wood, conveyed an illusion of a wood on fire. The wind had risen, and when for a moment the echo of gun fire ceased in the wood the trees moaned in the wind as if men were crying out in pain. We picked our way through disused trenches and shell-holes towards the spinney. Near us the great flares rose and fell between the opposing lines. The calm radiance of the moon healed the gaping scars of day, but threw over all an atmosphere illusive and unreal. Man seemed very puny, his life very fugitive. The moon had shed its light on these woods and fields above the Ancre long before man had come into the world. It would do so long after he had gone. What cared eternal forces for man, his hopes and his fears?

We reached the spinney safely, and made our way towards the front line. Then, as I had anticipated, we reaped our reward for neglecting the beaten path of the communication trench. There was a tumult of vivid flashes and explosions. I flung myself down. Silence ensued, broken by the voice of the sergeant asking the sapper if he was hurt. Although the shells had burst all round us, we had providentially escaped, and we passed on to Johnstone's Post and found our working party. As soon as we arrived there was a rushing sound like the sudden uprising of a storm, and some light shells passed just over us and exploded in a trench beyond. Through the night the shells came at frequent intervals, but always just overshot their mark. The men worked on unheeding, and at last the order came to return home. A little while later I had seen the last of my men disappear into a cellar in the ruins of Authuille, and thrusting aside the blanket which was the door of my dug-out, found my company commander still awake, with a tale of heavy shelling throughout the night. When morning came we found blissfully reposing on the frail roof of the dug-out a heavy shell which had fortunately proved to be of defective design.

The near approach of the battle redoubled the calls on the infantry for fatigue parties, and in the last days we knew little rest. In the line the incessant shell fire and unrelenting vigilance deprived us of rest by day or night ; in support we were constantly called out on working parties. At Blackhorse Bridge we paraded at 8 in the morning for day working parties, returning in the late afternoon. At 8 in the evening we went out again, returning at dawn. Officers and men grew desperately tired, and the prospect of attack which could not but terminate in a period of rest became more than ever alluring. There were times when the constant deprivation of sleep drove men almost out of their mind. Their speech became incoherent and their movements mechanical. Once after five nights of continuous duty, with only a few hours of rest during the day, I found myself discussing with a sergeant the arrangements which I proposed to make for the execution of my sergeant-major, a man for whom I had the highest regard. To keep one's eyelids from descending in such circumstances of fatigue was among the most painful of experiences. Fortunately even fatigue knows a "second wind," for it was not till four days later that I sank happily on to the wire bed of a dug-out and removed my boots for the first time in nine days.

Yet one man found considerable satisfaction in this life. He was an officer in a pioneer battalion and by rights should have lived in a comfortable encampment in a wood behind the lines. He had, however, at one time contrived to secure a dug-out in the vicinity of the front line, and some mysterious duties. There he remained in a state of great happiness, sending notes, we were informed, to his colonel protesting against the suggestion that he might be relieved. I visited him one day with my company commander, and, knowing him to be a religious man, decided that he must be a descendant of one of those sturdy followers of Cromwell, who went to war chanting "a holy and a cheerful note."

Such was the incomparable tedium and weariness of the fatigues that the intermittent fighting came rather as a relief. Crawling one morning down the shallowest of trenches, I reached at last a shell-hole in which the night before an advanced post had been established. The shell-hole was deep and was occupied by a lance-corporal and three men. Movement of any sort was out of the question; to reveal that the shell-hole was tenanted could not but bring destruction on all. A day of complete leisure was therefore before them, and rarely have I seen men so contented. Before leaving I observed to the lance-corporal in an undertone that the position which he held was one of great danger, and wholly isolated, to which he replied in the Dorset dialect that he would be all right so long as he did not lose his pipe. I crawled away well satisfied to belong to a county whose ancient motto is " *Who's Afeard?* "

To be confined with another man in a shell-hole gives rise to many ludicrous happenings; inevitably the conversation turns on the chances of a " better 'ole." I remember another occasion at night, when my company commander, Kestell Cornish, and I were peacefully occupying a shell-hole which had fortunately presented itself at the moment when a German machine-gunner had got our direct line. The stream of bullets raged without ceasing over the shell-hole with the sound of whiplashes. Suddenly two Highlanders fell on top of us, and proceeded to engage each other in a conversation, apparently of a humorous character, but virtually unintelligible. We took advantage of a momentary respite to leave the two Highlanders, still amusing each other immensely. I observed on occasion that tranquillity made the Highlanders dour and morose, while action produced in them an invincible gaiety. I remember being driven nearly wild on a somewhat hazardous working party in advance of our lines, when silence was of vital importance, by the continuous clinking of spades and exchanges of pawky humour, which the Highlanders appeared to regard as inseparable from the digging of an advanced trench under fire.

There was grim and confused fighting one night before Thiepval. The Ulster Division, who were on our left, had planned a small operation, preceded by a barrage. A little before our barrage was due to commence a whirlwind bombardment opened on our line, gradually concentrating on the company next the Ulstermen. Our trenches and outpost positions were levelled. Many of our men were killed and wounded, while others were buried in the débris. All four companies were in the front line, and the battalion in support was too far away to come into action in time. There was some confusion, as is inevitable when arrangements for attack have hurriedly to be adjusted to defence. An hour after the commencement of the barrage the Germans attacked in force. They were driven off except at one point where our trenches had ceased to exist; here there was hand-to-hand fighting in which the company commander and a corporal, though seriously wounded, contrived to take part, supporting each other back to back.

Meanwhile the barrage was raging on battalion headquarters at Johnstone's Post and the communication trenches, denying any chance of effective support. Orderly after orderly was sent out, but every man was killed or wounded before he had gone a dozen yards. The sergeant-major went out to collect what men he could find and entered a dug-out. There were several men apparently sitting round a table. He ordered them out. There was no reply. They were all dead, killed by the concussion of a heavy shell.

One element of humour was provided by a German who had repented of his martial enthusiasm and used a map, with which he had been supplied, to make his way to the headquarters of a neighbouring company. The commander of the company was surprised, and a little disconcerted, by his arrival; but the German set his doubts at rest with a pleasant smile. Then he produced from his pockets a handful of buttons, which with characteristic thoroughness he had collected from his comrades before setting out, and offered them as an expression of his goodwill. The company commander reported that he was a man of pleasant manners and peaceable disposition.

My company was not implicated in the hand-to-hand fighting with bomb and bayonet, but was brought in from the right in relief of the much-attenuated company which had been most engaged. The position was one of some anxiety. The trench line, and such wire as had once protected it, had been destroyed. We were still without supports. And a warning was received from headquarters that another attack was imminent. But none came. This sector, however, remained most dangerous, and the reconstitution of a trench line out of the interlocking shell-holes was a matter of difficulty owing to the incessant shell fire. The German snipers were active, and a progress round our advanced posts became a hazardous proceeding. The Germans seemed content to leave much of the line alone, while concentrating all available guns and Minenwerfer on this sector.

The heavy shells were not so disturbing as the Minenwerfer bombs. The former came with a rushing sound and at a speed which made escape impossible. It was easy to adopt a fatalistic attitude in regard to them. The latter could just be discerned as they sailed through the sky, a nightmare of black blobs. By keeping unceasing vigilance one might avoid them. The temptation to keep this vigilance was considerable, as they annihilated anything within a few yards of their explosion. The strain of watching the flight of the bombs, combined with the appalling noise which often made speech impossible, and the constant deprivation of rest for many days on end, placed a great strain on the nerves. In practice the troops became so tired as to be indifferent and made little effort to safeguard themselves. The casualties were high. Day and night one was deprived of any chance of rest, or withdrawn from necessary work, by the cry of " Stretcher-bearer," and hurrying down the trench one would find a blown-in dug-out with men hastily digging out their comrades, who were usually past any such need. Once a bomb landed in the middle of a party of men who were engaged in getting their lunch out of a dixie, and even the oldest soldiers were on the verge of sickness when their duties compelled them to pass that way.

I left this sector one morning just after the last occurrence with orders to conduct some officers of the 25th Division, which was in corps reserve, round the line. I was so tired that I could hardly stand. I had been on my feet almost continuously throughout the preceding forty-eight hours in circumstances of considerable strain, and before that I had had several days and nights on duty. But the prospect of leaving this particular corner had in it elements of attraction. It was a long way to Aveluy down the communication trenches and along the Ancre. But the day was glorious; the meadows and woods were beautiful in the sunlight; and the river reminded me of the river which passed my home. The garden of the Château of Aveluy where I had to wait for my party was aglow with roses. As I sat there it came to my mind that the wheel had come full circle within a few hours. What could be more horrible than the blood-soaked trench which I had left in the early morning, more beautiful than this garden with its background of sunlit woods and river?

At length the officers arrived in an omnibus. I led them along the Ancre, unfolding the local history and gossip, and came to the end of the communication trench. There was some discussion here, but I fortunately closed it in the nick of time, as the German gunners, ever on the alert, opened fire on us with a battery of light guns. A little later I saw a Minenwerfer bomb coming right at us. The officers, who came from a part of the line quieter than Thiepval, were less observant. I shouted " Down at once ! " and had the pleasure of observing a colonel and three captains carrying out the order of a second lieutenant with the " instant, implicit, and unquestioning obedience " enjoined by the Field Service Regulations, and following his excellent example. No one was hurt, but there was a distinct disposition afterwards to hurry, a disposition which I encouraged, being anxious to get a little rest before the night came when no man might sleep.

Such are a few of my memories of the fighting above the Ancre, and already they seem very distant. For many years no sound of gun fire has echoed through the trees of Aveluy and Thiepval Woods. They echo only to the passing of trains along those lines which then were overgrown with weeds. Not yet have all traces of war been obliterated; so heavy was the fighting here that the scars will remain to the end of time. For many years to come stray travellers will revisit the ground where once they fought and endured, where many of their friends lie for ever. But the time must come when the travellers are seen no more, and only the forest of graves above the Ancre will remain to tell the tale of that island race whose sons once were lords of these woods and fields.

CHAPTER IX

THE MARSHES OF THE YSER

THE Dorsets went north to Givenchy, then a quiet part of the line, to rest after the early days of the Somme. They returned in November, greatly to distinguish themselves at the battle of Serre Ridge. This battle was pre-eminently a soldier's battle; it assumed almost the character of personal combat.

The fortress villages of Serre and Beaumont-Hamel had been the scene of the grimmest carnage of the first day of the Somme; an attack by three divisions in November had gained possession of Beaumont-Hamel and part of the forward trench system. In weather which had finally broken and in face of German reserves newly brought into the battle, the 14th Infantry Brigade advanced to the assault of the Serre and Munich trench systems.

The previous attacks had created a situation of some confusion; British and German posts were established in no ordered line amid a wilderness of shell-holes and ruined trenches. In the confusion an error was made in the artillery barrage; it fell short and caused heavy casualties in the attacking troops. Undaunted, the 2nd Manchesters formed up in advance of the barrage and went forward, winning by the hardest fighting Serre trench. The attack withered before the uncut wire of Munich trench, but one company effected a lodgment. There they fought to the last; their bodies were discovered months later grouped round the barricades which they had built and defended with such gallantry. Meanwhile the Dorsets came up in support and consolidated the ground won. Into this soldiers' battle, my company sergeant-major, Jim Miller, led A Company after the loss of all its officers, closing a gap between two battalions and saving a situation which but for his presence of mind and superb resolution and leadership could not have been retrieved. Unable to dig in the knee-deep mud, and refusing to fall back, the Dorsets established posts with any material which came to hand. " Hope Post," the scene of most bitter fighting, was a breastwork built of British and German dead; as each man died he was added to the breastwork by his surviving comrades. Here for six days and nights they fought with bomb, rifle, and bayonet, far in advance of our lines. Isolated by a sea of mud swept without ceasing by artillery and machine-gun fire, receiving no orders, no rations, and no ammunition, the Dorsets fought on under the command of a subaltern, H. C. Butcher, who already wore the ribbon of the Distinguished Service Order won at Leipzig Redoubt. They drew their rations and ammunition from the thronging dead; they drank the polluted water in the shell-holes. For five days the wounded could not be evacuated. They crawled, if they could, to the shattered dug-outs to lie, until death came to their release, amid an inchoate mass of dying and dead. When at last a carrying party of another battalion, led by a captain of the R.A.M.C., succeeded under cover of a fog in reaching the forward area, they were able to sort out but a few still living; these few were drawn from eight battalions. So ended 1916.

The frustrate hopes of 1917 constitute in the minds of many soldiers the darkest memories of the war. Notwithstanding the heavy casualties and long-drawn-out fighting of the Somme, the morale of the Army was as high in the spring of 1917 as it has ever been. The chivalrous ardour of the early days had passed, but in its place there had come a grim resolution which was as sure an earnest of victory. Those who had fought across the wilderness of shell-holes filled with human wreckage which lay around Thiepval, Guillemont, and a score of other villages on the Somme were not likely to have many illusions as to the price of victory. Yet there was a belief that the breakdown of the weather in the autumn had alone prevented a decisive success, and that the increase in our strength, both in men and in guns, and the opportunity of taking the offensive early in the year, would make victory inevitable. The year started well for my regiment with an action at Cépy Farm, near St. Quentin, which earned for it the thanks of the commanders of the 4th and 5th Armies and of the Commander-in-Chief. The order of the day, signed by General Lumsden, who won the Victoria Cross, stated that " the dash with which your battalion attacked and the tenacity with which it has held on to Cépy Farm under intense and continuous artillery bombardment are not only object-lessons to us all, but are in accordance with the highest traditions of the British Army." St. Quentin lay, a tempting prize, below; the Germans were for the moment demoralised. The men were eager to continue the attack, but the Staff, knowing well that the devastated country to the west precluded the arrival of supporting troops and guns in adequate numbers, would not countenance any further advance.

Shortly afterwards news arrived of the great success of the first day of the Battle of Arras. The Canadians on the left, and Scottish and English divisions on the right, stormed the heights of Vimy which had remained in German hands after the great French offensive in Artois two years before. Few can have anticipated that the splendid *élan* of the spring of 1917 would have earned no higher reward than the crests of Vimy and Messines and an area of a few square miles in the vicinity of Ypres reduced by shell fire to a vast and noisome swamp.

At no time in the war was the morale of the Army more near to breaking than in the carnage of the Third Battle of Ypres. The war of attrition had few advocates among those who were enabled to judge its merits, and the extent of its success, in the abomination of desolation which stretched from Houthulst Forest to Passchendaele. Here men picked their way under withering shell fire towards the forward area along duck-board tracks between shell-holes. The wounded fell into shell-holes and were drowned in their fœtid depths. In the forward area, where the duck-board tracks could not penetrate, men floundered in and out of shell-holes, vainly seeking to keep their feet, in the wake of a creeping barrage, which, however slow it crept, was soon far ahead. In October the provisional orders for an advance in the direction of Westroosebeke gave my company eight minutes for every 100 yards, but even this pace proved in the course of the month to be far beyond the capacity of men in the prevailing conditions. The shortest advance was bought at the price of heavy casualties and complete exhaustion. In June of 1916 I had drawn for the benefit of my company a picture of the forward sweep of the British and French Armies on the Somme, and of the Russians in the east, with Victory at the end of the year. In the autumn of 1917 I could tell them only that their rôle was " to kill, kill, and keep on killing " till at some date, which no one now cared to forecast, a collapse of the German morale should set in.

The true facts of the situation might be concealed from those at home by the reiteration of success in every Press announcement; they could not be concealed from those who had first-hand evidence of the cost at which half a dozen pill-boxes and a few hundred yards of swamp were bought. The later stages of the battle could only have been fought by an army so well disciplined as to be content to be sacrificed for reasons which could not be deduced from the military situation patent to their eyes. It is to the credit of the citizen armies of Great Britain and the Dominions that in the course of three years they had achieved such a discipline. It is some consolation to them to-day to know that the continuance of the Third Battle of Ypres in the late autumn of 1917 was ordered for political as much as for military reasons, and that the " steady, grim, despairing ranks" who struggled forward inch by inch, till at last a ruin reported to have been known once by the name of Passchendaele fell into their hands, saved the Allies from political disruption and defeat.

Yet hope came when it was least expected, and set men thinking of what might have been, had the strategy of 1917 taken another course. Late in November, in a hospital peopled for the most part by the wounded of Passchendaele, the calm of the evening was disturbed by two new arrivals. One was a very young subaltern of infantry, slightly wounded in the arm; the other a veteran in the Tanks, with a bandaged head. "Ypres?" we inquired casually. "No," the answer came; "down south near Cambrai." "Did you pass the hundred yard mark?" "A hundred yards!" echoed the subaltern scornfully. "I went the better part of three miles, and I was the first man in the battalion to be hit." The wounded of a less happy occasion laughed grimly and turned to the tank commander for more authentic news. But his experience had been less fortunate. He spoke of the gathering of the tanks in the shelter of the great wood, and their successful advance over line after line of trenches. He described the advance of the Highland Territorials in the wake of the tanks, their casual bearing as they emerged from our trenches, their hands in their pockets and their rifles slung, their onslaught with the bayonet on the German front line, and their subsequent reappearance a little while afterwards, each with a looted cigar in his mouth, but otherwise still bearing a contemptuous and quite unruffled appearance, until the occurrence of another line of trenches required a further recourse to their bayonets. He told also the story of a German artillery officer, the last survivor of his battery, who single-handed served his gun and knocked out tank after tank as they came over a rise near Flesquières. The tank commander had himself been wounded by a direct hit on his tank by this gunner. This did not in any way affect his admiration for a man whose superb courage and resolution turned the fortunes of the day, and whose memory is still honoured, though his name is unknown, by the soldiers of two nations. At last the infantry closed on him, and would have spared his life, but he refused to surrender, and was killed at the gun which he had served so well.

The circumstances of infantry fighting in the war were not such as to engender a chivalrous attitude towards the enemy; indeed, a sustained chivalry existed only in the clean warfare carried on in the air. But there were occasions when a superb act of courage received as much honour from foe as from friend. I have been told by an officer of the Machine-gun Corps that on the first day of Arras he reached the limit of our advance and found that it was held up by a German gunner firing over open sights. At last the gunner was surrounded and, still in the act of firing his gun, was killed. Late that night, when this line still represented the farthest limit of advance, and the position was one of the utmost danger, he was going round his posts when he found that some of his men had ceased for a few minutes from consolidating their position. They were burying the German gunner, alone of all the dead around.

It is on record also that when Ovillers surrendered, after sixteen days of bomb and bayonet fighting in its ruins, the British troops came to the salute as the small remnant of the German garrison passed through to our lines. Yet these instances were so rare as to pale into insignificance before the number of deeds of violence done by angry men, whose experiences had filled their hearts with cold fury and disgust. Chivalry could hardly survive in the desolate swamps which lay north of Ypres and the Yser Canal.

Yet it was on the Yser in 1917 that we spent some of the most interesting, and latterly some of the most quiet, days during the war. Certain divisions were chosen to carry out an attack of a particularly hazardous character on the Belgian coast. The attack was to be a combined operation with the Navy on the one part and with the Fifth and Second Armies before Ypres on the other. A small area of polder and dune, stretching from the mouth of the Yser, which was here canalised, to the village of St. Georges, was taken over from the French by the 1st and 32nd Divisions in preparation for this enterprise. It was reported that the 1st Division were in quarantine owing to an infectious disease, but it was understood that they were in fact undergoing a course of aquatics and were in the hands of swimming instructors.

The Germans were not deceived, and early in July put in a counter-offensive in anticipation of our attack, and at a time when our guns were not in position and our troops were unfamiliar with the terrain. No more admirable place for a minor offensive could have been chosen. The bridgehead of Nieuport was of a reasonable size and was protected by Vauban's Redan, a great earthwork honeycombed by passages and deep dug-outs in which a battalion could be concealed and move freely from one position to another in complete immunity from shell fire. Fifteen-inch shells occasionally put out the lights, but shells of smaller calibre almost escaped notice. But the approaches to the redan led over the locks of the canalised Yser and crossed five bridges in quick succession. These bridges were destroyed by gun fire, the front line being but a few hundred yards distant, on the smallest evidence of activity on our part, and the sapper company charged with their maintenance suffered casualties far in excess of those of the infantry. To the west of Nieuport our front line ran in the sand-dunes on the north bank of the Yser. To the east the line reached no farther than the towpath on the far bank of the canal, and the barrel bridges by which it was approached were commanded by German machine-gun posts established on both banks of the canal.

Two battalions of the 1st Division (the Northamptons and the 60th Rifles) held the sand-dunes west of Nieuport on the morning of July 10; the bridgehead of Nieuport and the redan were held by the 32nd Division. A bombardment of great intensity destroyed every bridge and isolated all the battalions north of the Yser. An attack followed. The battalions of the 1st Division, cut off from any chance of retreat and with no room in which they could manœuvre, set themselves to sell their lives at the highest cost. When night came, four officers and seventy men swam the Yser and came safely to our lines; they were all who remained. The 32nd Division, though isolated, had more room to manœuvre, and after heavy fighting all day around Vauban's Redan, this magnificent earthwork and the bridgehead of Nieuport were still in our hands. Vauban can hardly have anticipated that his redan would have rendered its most notable service to France in the year 1917.

After July 10 this sector became relatively quiet. The thunder of the guns to the east spoke of the great battles raging before Ypres. The Germans had no men to spare for minor enterprises, and showed little disposition to press the advantage which they had gained. Their troops in the line were the least combative of any in my experience, and, notwithstanding the security of their own positions and the exposed character of the British lines, they appeared to want nothing better than to be left alone. No attack was in fact made by the 1st and 32nd Divisions. Matters progressed so ill in the Flanders offensive that the main strategic plan of freeing the Belgian coast was abandoned. In the autumn the divisions destined to take part in this enterprise found their way to the swamps near Westroosebeke, where their training for amphibious warfare stood them in good stead.

In the meantime there was much that was new and interesting in the dune and polder country to troops who had grown weary of the grey and monotonous landscape of Flanders and the vast expanses of ravaged countryside which lay between the Hindenburg line and the old front line of 1916. Nieuport was not greatly different from other towns lying in the near vicinity of the front line. Nieuport Bains, a summer resort lying at the mouth of the Yser and adorned by the usual gimcrack villas, was levelled nearly to the ground and the other " bains " which occurred down the coast line were much bespattered by shell fire. War seemed more than usually odd as one sat in some convenient fold of the dunes and watched the waves lapping the belts of wire on the shore and the play of machine guns over the sands where but a short while before men and women had kept holiday and children had built sand-castles.

But the sand-dunes did not show the traces of shell fire in the same degree as the chalk country of the Somme. Shells exploding in the sand appeared to be choked in the loose texture and to have a limited effect. I observed a heavy shell explode one day in our horse lines between two rows of picketed horses. I expected most of the horses to be hit, but no horse was touched, and the shell-hole was of small dimensions.

It was perhaps as well that the effect of gun fire was limited, as the German coast defence batteries included many guns of the heaviest calibre. These ranged generally on Vauban's Redan before Nieuport, and on Dunkirk and Malo les Bains, which, though twenty-three miles away, were hardly less dangerous than the forward area on account of shell fire and incessant bombing attack by the German squadrons. On occasion, however, the heavy batteries turned their attention on the infantry rest camps. I was particularly irritated one evening, on coming into such a camp, to find a shell-hole of the most recent origin, in which a haystack could have been concealed, on the site of my resting-place for the night. On another occasion, when in close support in a farm behind Nieuport and at a time when I was enjoying my tea, there was a deafening crash such as I had never heard before, and a huge fountain of black smoke rose to a great height some hundred yards away. I went outside to investigate and met a gunner officer. " A large shell, that," I observed. " Very large," replied the gunner. " Fifteen inch ? " I queried. " Oh, no, much larger than that." " I suppose that they are aiming at the farm," I continued. " I don't see what else they can be aiming at." Receiving no comfort I retired to my interrupted tea, soon afterwards to receive the reassuring news that the fountain of black smoke proceeded from the explosion of a dump of some million rounds of small-arm ammunition on which the German gunners had scored a direct hit.

The country to the east of the dunes was low-lying polder. The fields, trim and orderly, were intersected by innumerable ditches, full of water, rendering the movement of men difficult in the daytime and well-nigh impossible at night, except on the roads. On the right of the British line in the vicinity of the village of St. Georges the country had been flooded in 1914 when the Belgians opened their dykes in order that one small strip of Belgium might still remain inviolate. The flooded country was traversed only by the high towpaths of the Yser Canal and by a number of causeways and duck-board tracks. The defences took the form of breastworks and strong points constructed of concrete or fashioned out of the ruins of the farms.

An active enemy could have made life intolerable in these marshes. The breastworks were inadequate and often unprotected from the rear. The causeways which led to them were few and wholly exposed. The German lines lay in an arc round the Nieuwland Polder and the village of St. Georges, enabling their machine-gunners to fire at short range either in enfilade or from the rear down most of the causeways and breastworks. Bullets appeared to come from all sides. The most exposed part of the line was the towpath on the far bank of the canal. The line ran here in an easterly direction for 1,300 yards until a post was reached where it ended. It was then resumed on the near bank and ran south. The Germans had machine-gun posts within a short distance of our line on each bank and could fire in direct enfilade down the canal, effectually denying any chance of reinforcement of the troops on the far bank. The frail bridges of barrels lashed together, which represented the only means of approach, were dangerous to cross in the darkest hour of the night. In the daytime, and at times of serious activity, they could be rendered impassable. It was always an interesting problem to judge the correct pace for a successful crossing. If a man went too fast, the barrels lurched to one side or the other and projected him into the canal. If he went too slow, the German machine-gunners caught him. The approaches to the bridges were aptly named " Nasty Avenue " and " Nasty Walk."

Security was, however, conferred in some measure by the inactivity of the Germans and by the mist which rose from the swamps soon after sunset. Even on a moonlit night the ground visibility extended only for a short distance. On many nights the mist was so thick that it was difficult to see more than a few yards. Posts were far apart, and it was easy to lose one's way on the causeways connecting them. On the first night when I went round my posts I went alone, and although I had reconnoitred them in the daytime I was soon compelled to admit that I had lost all sense of direction, and from time to time I arrived at a post not knowing whether it was tenanted by friend or foe. The causeways were composed of narrow duck-boards, and when they were swept by machine guns it was impressed on my mind that a man, however lightly wounded, would probably fall into the marsh and be no more seen. I felt very lonely, and there was something uncanny in the chance sights and sounds which came out of the mist. The stuttering of the machine guns blended weirdly with the cries of the wildfowl, while the boom of distant naval guns and the muffled screech of the great shells passing far overhead were punctuated by the rhythmic throb of giant bombing aeroplanes on their way to Bruges or Dunkirk. In the mist also men passed as shadowy forms, and ruined buildings suddenly loomed up and as soon disappeared. Of these the most strange was the ruined Chapel of St. Georges. I had a sense that I had seen it before, and later it came to my mind that Tennyson had conceived just such a scene for the " last weird battle in the

West," fought by the remnant of the Knights of the Table Round.

> A death-white mist slept over sand and sea,
> Whereof the chill, to him who breathed it, drew
> Down with his blood, till all his heart was cold
> With formless fear ; and even on Arthur fell
> Confusion, since he saw not whom he fought,
> For friend and foe were shadows in the mist.

The chapel of St. Georges, which seemed to me so familiar, was the chapel nigh the field to which Arthur was borne :

> A broken chancel with a broken cross,
> That stood on a dark strait of barren land,
> On one side lay the Ocean, and on one
> Lay a great water, and the moon was full.

There were certain disadvantages in living on barren land surrounded by a great water. It was impossible to dig down more than a few inches, and the French had buried their dead where they fell. The mist spoke of fever, and the fauna at all times to be found in trenches here attained a number and a virulence which were admitted by all (even by one of my subalterns who had been on Gallipoli) to be without parallel in their experience. My wrists, for which the mosquitoes had a particular predilection, were so covered by bites that they became swollen and shapeless. The immediate result was to reduce my vitality and to make me easily tired.

I discovered this one night when I was

making my way down the long road which led from Nieuport to the south. It stretched interminably before me; in the canal which bordered it the moon, blood-red in the enshrouding mist, was reflected, accompanying me on my way. I became more and more weary, and at last was on the point of giving up, when I heard far away in the mist the sound of the *Marseillaise*. I was suitably impressed and moved forward again on my way; the phenomenon was explained later when a platoon of Highlanders emerged, a group of shadowy forms, only to disappear again into the mist ahead. On another occasion I was overcome by fever in the earliest stages of a march of twelve miles. I could hardly see the ground at my feet, but I was able mechanically to keep pace with the man in front. It was not, however, an easy matter, and when the march ended I collapsed.

But the casualties, other than from sickness, in the Yser marshes were few. The regiment was in good heart and undismayed by the failure of the 1917 offensive and the prospect of another winter in Flanders. When a dangerous enterprise was planned, every subaltern in the regiment submitted an application to be placed in charge of it. A company commander advanced the technical point that his promotion had not appeared in the *London*

Gazette, and he was therefore still the senior subaltern, with a traditional right to claim the leadership of such enterprises. His claim was upheld, but he became the object of as much dislike on the part of the other subalterns as if he had cheated at cards.

Among the men in A Company, which I now commanded, there were still a few who had survived three years of constant fighting and had now before them a fourth winter of war, with all its attendant misery and exposure. Two of my old platoon sergeants, Home and Stevens, had become company sergeant-majors of other companies. I had still Jim Miller, the most sturdy and reliable of sergeant-majors. I thought it right to ask him to apply for a commission in the regular army, though I could hardly contemplate the loss of his support in maintaining the reputation of the company. I was more than grateful to him when he said that he would not take a commission so long as I was in command of the company. Not least among my many reasons for regretting the ill-fortune which cut short my command of A Company is that Jim Miller applied for and immediately obtained a commission, and died, a subaltern in the South Staffords, north of the Somme on the darkest day of March 1918.

These " Old Contemptibles " had not lost heart. One night I found beyond the Yser one of my sergeants throwing sand-bags on to a breastwork. I ascertained that he regarded himself as still " in the pink." He informed me that he could manage everything except the long marches, but that this did not really matter, as the colonel allowed him to come up to the trenches in an ambulance or any transport available. This man was well over military age, and had caused much entertainment in the early days of the war. His son, who was too young for the Army, had enlisted by the simple expedient of overstating his age. The sergeant was furious and ordered him to return home to look after his mother. The son very properly drew attention to the fact that his father was over age and that it was his duty to look after his wife. But discipline was strong in that Dorset family, and the father remained in the Army while the son returned sorrowfully home, a statement of the son's iniquity having been duly communicated to the " proper authorities " by his indignant parent.

The exchange, moreover, of fraternal greetings with the Belgian army on our right was an unfailing source of amusement. The Dorsets shared the common illusion of the forces in France and Flanders that they were masters of the native tongue, and there were Belgians who were confident that they spoke English. The right-hand post of the British Army lay on the bank of a canal known as the Groot Beverdyk Vaart; on the far side of the canal was a Belgian post. Communication was maintained by a barrel attached by a rope to each bank. One moonlit night I was standing with some Dorsets looking over the canal when a Belgian made signs on the far bank which were interpreted to mean that he wished to fraternise. He seated himself on the barrel and was pulled across. Landing with some difficulty, he rose to his full height, saluted me and said, " 'Ello, my boy! Me speak Eengleesh." I cast a stern glance at my Dorsets, but it was unnecessary. The natural courtesy of the men of Wessex prevented any demonstration louder than a smile.

My knowledge of French was little better than the Belgian's knowledge of English, and within a short time the barrel was again proceeding on its precarious way to the opposite bank. Indeed, on looking over old letters I gather that much of my time was devoted to making myself understood, and I find constant reports of conversations with the natives which did not lead to any satisfactory result. Being ignorant of the French for honey, I appear to have asked for the " confiture du bee," adding by way of explanation (unhappily to no purpose) " un petit volant la fait, comme ça."

It is of interest to read letters written at the front, as in some degree they reveal what was the reaction of one's mind day by day to the abnormal life occasioned by the war, and they correct the impression which now remains, distorted by many years of secure and normal life. It is very clear that nearly every day contained something diverting; indeed, a casual reader would deduce that the great variety of humorous incidents was the main feature of life at the front. I seem to have had about this time a misfortune owing to a colonel evicting a subaltern from a tent known as Villa Mon Désir during the night. Arriving shortly after dawn, I made an effort to rouse the supposed subaltern, and my language worsened steadily until a grizzled figure appeared in pyjamas. " Luckily," the letter concludes, " it is a foggy morning."

It is strange, in reading these letters, to recall to mind the circumstances in which many of them were written. At this time I had a strange premonition that my days were numbered, and this premonition developed into certainty one day when I had occasion to acquire a duty which seemed to me, from an intimate knowledge of the circumstances, to confer no chance of survival on the leader, and little, if any, chance on the men with him. I remember passing down a duck-board track in the afternoon, and reflecting, as I watched the sunshine on the marshes, how death, once so strange and terrible, had become almost a matter of routine. A dead man lay outside the door of my headquarters dug-out, waiting till night should come and he might safely be taken away. He excited no more attention than if he had been asleep. When the lives of all were forfeit, the prospect of losing one's life before another dawn did not present itself as a great misfortune. I must have written a letter that evening, yet it is not identifiable; nor indeed are other letters at that time concerned with any but trivial matters, except one letter in which there is a statement: "I am as eager now as then" (referring to 1915), and another which contains a cryptic remark: "Victory is sure, but we will have to pay a heavy price for it." In the event I survived that occasion because our line was unexpectedly taken over by another battalion during the early part of the night.

A few days later I enjoyed my twenty-first birthday in Dunkirk. There were two restaurants open in that much-bombed city. I was billeted in a suburb, and my progress towards the centre of the town through its dark and untenanted streets was punctuated by a rain of bombs from a squadron of German aeroplanes overhead. The distance to the nearest aerodrome being some thirty miles, bombing was continuous all night, and every night, at this time, and each aeroplane was able to drop four bombs at a time. Night in Dunkirk was one long thunderstorm, without the rain, and even that effect was not always lacking, as it was very easy in the darkness to walk into one of the many canals. I reached, however, the Place Jean Bart and went to ground in the restaurant to wait for my friend, Robin Kestell Cornish, with whom I had arranged to celebrate my coming of age. He did not turn up, having failed to get my message. I had accordingly a rather melancholy meal with half a bottle of cheap claret in lieu of the promised champagne. I returned in due time to my billet and went to bed in an attic. I awoke a little later and thought that the night was unusually noisy, even for Dunkirk. I found next morning that the German navy had made a raid along the coast, and that the noise which had awakened me had been caused by the obliteration of the chimney-stack immediately above my attic. So ended my twenty-first birthday, and I recorded in a letter my great satisfaction that it had been spent out of the line. A more successful dinner appears to have taken place in Dunkirk. There was certainly enough to drink, and the wine fulfilled its traditional rôle of inducing the telling of the truth at last, for my letter concludes: " At the front the only thing to do is to live well and forget while you can. The most fatal mistake is to think at all."

CHAPTER X

DAWN ON ASIAGO

EDDYING clouds swept over the vast expanse of plain which lay between the mountains and the Adriatic, shrouding the Euganean hills and the cities and villages over which Venice had in time past held sway. Of late the tumult of war had desecrated this smiling countryside, and men of many nations had thronged the dusty roads. The Lion of St. Mark, still proudly erect in the Piazza of Vicenza, had looked down for many months on a motley array of uniforms, grey, khaki, and light blue, made yet more vivid by the distinguishing colours and emblems of rank or regiment, the kilts and glengarries of the Scottish regiments, the plumes of the Bersaglieri, the badges of the Alpini and Black Arditi, the dark headdresses of the Chasseurs Alpins. Now the tide of war which had beaten for so long against the barrier of the Piave lines had ebbed. But high on the Trentine Alps above the clouds the war did not seem far away. It was the morning of November 11, 1918, but news of the Armistice had not reached this remote corner of the far-flung battle line.

I made my way down the road through the great pine-woods towards our old front line, from which the 48th (South Midland) Division had advanced a few days before through the little town of Asiago, up the gorges of the Val d'Assa, and into a remote beyond. Through the trees I heard the familiar tramp of soldiers on the march, and I stood at the side of the road to watch the return of an infantry brigade from its last fight. For nearly four years this brigade had been on foreign service, in the mud of the Ypres salient, on the chalk uplands of Picardy, and latterly amid the rocks and pine-woods of the Asiago Plateau. The last of their battles was fought. This was the hour of victory, the long-awaited hour, the consummation of four years of unremitting toil and sacrifice. Yet on the faces of these men who had borne the burden and heat of the day I could discern neither triumph nor relief. Their faces were grey with the fatigue of many days of marching and fighting ; their uniforms were stained with mud and dust ; the burden of rifle, pack, and steel helmet which each man bore lay heavy on them. Their weariness of body was matched by a yet greater weariness in their eyes. Yet both in their eyes and in their bearing the dominant impression was one of dignity. These men had lived long in the Valley of the Shadow ; they had learned there to distinguish between the false and the true. Their eyes were free from illusion, yet in them there was nothing of bitterness. Their bearing was proud, but in it there was nothing of arrogance. Theirs was the considerate pride of the craftsman in the greatest of all crafts, that of life. Their apprenticeship to that craft had been long and arduous. It was ended. They were men.

The regiments passed by and disappeared into the pine-woods girdling the mountain road ; the tramp of their feet died away. Yet I can see them still, each with his heavy burden, and I can hear the rhythm of those marching feet. I see them sometimes as a South Midland brigade, but more often as the men of that generation, my own, who when offered the heaviest of burdens, in the creation of which they had had no share, accepted it uncomplaining and marched away, passing out of the sight of men. Perhaps some such thought was in the mind of the Commander-in-Chief when in his dispatch describing this memorable day he wrote :

> By the long road they trod with so much faith and with such devoted and self-sacrificing bravery we have arrived at victory, and to-day they have their reward.

We had our reward ; we have it still. I knew well, as I watched the regiments pass, what that reward was, for of late I had been reading *Songs before Sunrise.*

Unto each man his handiwork, unto each his crown,
    The just Fate gives;
Whoso takes the world's life on him and his own lays down,
    He, dying so, lives.
Whoso bears the whole heaviness of the wronged world's weight,
    And puts it by,
It is well with him suffering, though he face man's fate;
    How should he die?

The road led to the little town of Asiago, which was my destination, but I turned aside in the vicinity of a small chapel which had escaped destruction, though within a few yards of our front line, owing to the protection afforded by a steep bank. On the far side of the bank the battlefield of the Asiago Plateau came into full view; in the background was a range of mountains, cleft by the Val d'Assa. In the foreground were our trenches and barbed wire; on the wire the "heart-shaking jests of decay" were lolling. For no apparent reason desultory shots were still being fired from some quarter; a bullet flashed by me with the sound of a whiplash, as of old. I traversed "No Man's Land," eloquent still of battle, here derelict rifles and equipment, there a grey figure recumbent and unheeding of the coming of peace. A machine gun in the Austrian front line was trained on our lines; the belt of cartridges was partly fired. A jagged rent in an unfired cartridge showed where the bullet had passed which had silenced this gun for ever and had put out the light of a man's life.

Late that afternoon I returned through the woods and reached the hutment camp near Tattenham Corner, where the road passed over the summit of the range and by a series of traverses on the mountainside descended several thousand feet to the plain. News of the Armistice had arrived, but there was no sign of unusual animation. The clouds had settled on the mountains; a grey mist eddied to and fro, clinging to the huts and pine trees. Shadowy groups of men could be discerned, but they appeared to be engaged on the usual errands of camp life. There was nothing to distinguish this day from any other day in the past four years.

At Tattenham Corner my usual good fortune enabled me to intercept a lorry descending to the plain, and I arrived at a large village, at this time a railhead for the British and Italian forces on the mountains to the north. There was a considerable military population of "base details"; the civil population was there in force, supplemented by a considerable accession of camp followers of the traditional type. No one here had any occasion to be tired, and a merry evening was clearly in prospect.

I dined with several officers at the billet of the Town Major. Most of them wore the badges of infantry regiments and the insignia which spoke of wounds or long service at the front. The meal was strangely quiet, and the thoughts of some were perhaps wandering, as were mine, over the past four years. How like this dinner was to a thousand other dinners, in which the tradition, handed down by generations of army cooks, that an officer must have a four-course meal in the evening in any circumstances, had been faithfully observed. Soup, disguised bully beef, tinned fruit, sardine on toast—I had eaten it how often, and in what strange surroundings! Yet how different was the meal in every other way! There had been dinners which were the prelude to hazardous occasions; why had they been so merry, while this dinner, the prelude to secure and ordered existence, was so quiet? Could it be that the absence from our board of Death, so long our neighbour, and the arrival of Life, so long a stranger to us, was causing embarrassment? We had always disliked that dark figure at the table, but we had got to know him well. This bright presence was very welcome; but we did not know him yet, and he was reported to have odd ways. We would have felt more comfortable if we had had with us certain absent friends, people who had greeted the dark figure when he first arrived with an easy familiarity, had always got on well with him, slapped him on the back in moments of excitement; they were the people who would have put this new arrival at his ease, made the evening go, perhaps kept him in his place if he essayed any of his well-known practical jokes. What an evening it might have been if only they had been here!

Dinner over, we made our way towards the Officers' Club. An Italian band was occupied in playing the national anthems of the Allies, and there was a substantial amount of excitement, mostly contributed by the representatives of the Latin races. The few British soldiers contented themselves for the most part with carrying their officers on their shoulders round the square. There was a general sense that the tributes which were being paid to the British armies should meet with some response, and at last an officer was found willing to undertake the task. He was possibly not the most suitable, as he spoke no Italian, belonged to the non-combatant services, and was in a state of considerable exhilaration. He discharged his task, however, to the satisfaction of the crowd, and his references to the sacrifices which he had made during the war and to his wife and family in Lancashire drew tears from himself and a further instalment of the National Anthem from the Italian band.

A few days later, in circumstances of greater dignity, I paraded my command to read to them a Special Order of the Day. Many of them had been on active service for the major part of the war; several were regular soldiers and had taken part in battles so distant as to be almost forgotten—Mons, Marne, and the first Ypres. In a silence which had its origin as much in emotion as in discipline, I read those eloquent words in which the thanks of the nation were conveyed to the forces in the field :

> Between that date and this you have traversed a long and weary road. Defeat has more than once stared you in the face. Your ranks have been thinned again and again by wounds, sickness, and death, but your faith has never faltered, your courage has never failed, your hearts have never known defeat. With your allied comrades you have won the day.

Winter in the Lombardy Plain was bitterly cold, in marked contrast to the grilling heat which we had endured during the summer. The base at Arquata Scrivia, in which I found myself at the end of the year, was fog-bound and cheerless. A peculiar, and most unjust, scheme of demobilisation was in force, which decreed that men should be released in an order of priority determined by professions and trades instead of length of service, and conferred on married men with four years' service in the field the privilege of seeing the return home of boys in certain selected trades who had arrived at the war in the late autumn of 1918. The anger and discontent which were prevalent on the Western Front in the months following the Armistice were attributed to the inevitable reaction following on the strain of years of war. But the responsibility rested in a considerable measure on the distinguished authors of this scheme of demobilisation. It gave me, however, as a " student," the opportunity of early release from the army. I spent some days at a camp waiting for the demobilisation train among the most remarkable crowd of " students " who have ever confessed to that title. Two jockeys were conspicuous among them ; others whose acquaintance with the racecourse was evident had presumably seen themselves described in the Press as students of form, and, in the absence of any other occupation set out in the bulky official handbook, had selected this group as most nearly describing their means of livelihood. A puzzled agricultural labourer who had entered himself as a " farm assist." was reported to be proceeding home in the privileged category of chemists.

DAWN ON ASIAGO

On a bitter morning we marched to the station and boarded a ramshackle collection of outworn trucks which was described as a train. There was a carriage, with compartments for the officers, of the type now reserved for exhibition in museums, and a rapid survey enabled me to ascertain that one compartment, already occupied by the train adjutant, alone possessed a complete set of glass and seats on both sides. I felt that this compartment presented peculiar attractions for a journey of several days, in part through the Mont Cenis Tunnel and High Savoy, in mid-winter. The same thought occurred to a mining engineer from the Rand. We put our point of view to the train adjutant, who proved amenable, and remained in his excellent company until our arrival at Cherbourg some days later, in spite of frequent and determined efforts to dislodge us made by the train commandant. We invariably obeyed his orders, but the train had a lamentable habit of starting at the precise moment when our baggage was at last collected and preparations for moving had reached an advanced stage.

In other wars the departure of troops for active service, and their return home, has usually been the occasion of some ceremony or mark of appreciation, repugnant to a few, but a source of pleasure to many. The soldier of the Great War was denied any ceremony on his departure for the front for military reasons well understood and appreciated by all. The imagination of those in authority did not enable them to realise how much it would have meant to the soldier, not only at that time, but in the years to come, if he had been permitted to return to his county or town with his battalion, the band at the head playing the old familiar tunes, his comrades by his side. A scheme by which composite battalions of soldiers with a certain length of service belonging to the same regiment were collected at demobilisation camps and sent home as units could not have been more cumbrous than the group scheme, and the industrial needs of the country, which apparently led to the adoption of that scheme, could have been met by the early demobilisation of the battalions drawn from the industrial areas most in need of labour. The return home had been much in the thoughts of the soldier; little did he expect that it would take the form ultimately decreed, and that he would be handed a railway ticket and be told to get out of his uniform as soon as possible. The arrival of the train by which I travelled from Southampton to Wimbledon was greeted by two girls, who loitered for a few moments on the bridge and waved a hand. We marched to the demobilisation camp, attracting not the smallest notice. Long before dawn the next morning I found myself in charge of my last parade. I gave for the last time the familiar orders; the men disappeared into the cold and darkness. I returned to the mess-room and sat by the fire. I had several hours to wait, but I had no desire to sleep again. In my last hours as a soldier I wanted to think, and in the firelight the memorable years marched by.

I saw a heather moor in southern England, the train throbbing into unknown night, the cliffs of Dover fading into the sea, the wilderness of white tents of the great base camp, the road by the sand-dunes of Etaples, the French labourer in his blouse silhouetted against the sunset on the railway singing the *Marseillaise* as the troops passed by, the muddy Lys, the gloom of a Flanders twilight, the march of tired men on the long road from Steenwerck to the south, and the warm glow of the braziers in the farm near Bois Grenier where at last it ended.

The scene moved to the Somme. I heard the thunder of the guns, the roar and echo of the heavy shells in the ruins of Albert. I saw the fitful moonlight among the ruins of Albert Cathedral, the dark walls of the château mess and the faces in the candlelight, the ghastly desolation and all-pervading mud of La Boisselle, the trees rent into strange shapes, the mine craters round the riven cemetery and the untouched cross, the barbed wire dark against the snow, the rank grass swaying mournfully in the wind, the coming of a winter dawn.

The Great Bear rose to the north above the dark mass of Thiepval Wood. The trees echoed endlessly to the crash of bombs and the staccato clamour of machine guns. The uplands beyond from Beaumont-Hamel to Serre were ablaze with the lurid light of a night bombardment. The air was shrill with the passing shells. The mill of Authuille stood sentinel above the flooded whispering Ancre. The marshes were aglow in the sunset. It was night; the glare of the Verey lights descending over No Man's Land illumined the stark ruins of Thiepval Château. Mouquet Farm gleamed in the sunlight at the end of the valley. The chalk parapets of Leipzig Redoubt lay but a short distance away. Nightmare days and nights succeeded each other, dominated by the torment of unceasing shell fire.

The scene moved north again. I saw the waves lapping the belts of wire on the Belgian shore, the moonlight on the Yser marshes, the mist rising from the lagoons and swamps, the ghostly forms, the lonely causeways, the broken chancel of St. Georges. I heard the stuttering machine guns blending weirdly with the cries of the wild fowl and the giant shells from the naval guns far overhead amid the bombing aeroplanes on their way to Bruges. I saw the long road leading from Nieuport to the south, and the longer road which led to Ypres.

The scene changed once more. I ascended the Trentine Alps up to and beyond the clouds, and standing among the giant boulders looked far over the Venetian plain, seeing from time to time a straggling village through a rift in the clouds, and the tops of mountains scattered far and wide like dream islands in a forgotten sea. To the north lay rocks ending in pine-woods. Where the pines ended lay the front line, and ruined Asiago beyond. I watched a brigade marching back from its last fight.

How much I had seen in these first years of manhood! What strange and wayward experiences had been mine! How much of the infinite variety of human nature, of the depths of the human heart, had been revealed to me, who had lived on terms of intimacy with men from the four corners of the world, who had known the comradeship of five nations in arms! No longer could I think of men in terms of profession, class, or creed. I had other and truer standards by which I might judge my fellow-men; I had with them a bond of union, a bond of common experience and common humanity, forged in the fires of war.

The tragic drama in which I had played an insignificant part was ended. Drama was said to purge the emotions through pity and fear. Now that the stage was empty, and the storm of emotion and conflict was stilled, it was time to reflect. What were these emotions of pity and fear? We watched a great drama on the stage. We saw man in conflict with forces beyond his control and overwhelmed. We were moved by sorrows greater than our own. Yet as the curtain fell we had not a less, but a greater, faith in that strange substance with which we were endued. We felt that we were greater than we knew. The frets of every day, our petty ambitions, the whips and scorns of time, were of less moment. Life was on a higher plane. We could almost see it whole.

Such was the influence of tragic drama on the stage. Had tragic experience a lesser power? Had the tragedy of the war taught humanity any lesson of abiding value? Was there any gain to set against apparent loss? Could anything atone for so much sorrow, such loss of young and splendid life? Could ancient hatreds die, and reconciliation come, as it came in Juliet's tomb, now that friend and foe, alike writ in sour misfortune's book, had been borne to a triumphant grave, and the youth of the world lay dead, " their vault a feasting presence full of light " ?

Were the hearts of men changed ? Many were broken ; some were bitter ; were any purged ? They had gone out into the dawn to meet death and had looked back on the setting sun over fields of carnage. They had lived for long in the shadow of death. They had seen, perhaps they had done, terrible things, deeds of violence and shame.

Yet there was another side to war : the evocation of noble qualities through generous service, the triumph of the spirit of man over disaster and death. How many men had gone to death as to a holiday and in the reckless generosity of youth had thrown away their lives " as 'twere a careless trifle " ! The more a man had to give, the more proudly and gladly did he give it. Hours of disaster had revealed the real greatness of men, and indeed of nations, and especially my own. The stubborn valour that was our proudest tradition had never risen to greater heights than in the desolate wastes of Passchendaele in the autumn of 1917, and on the Somme uplands in March of the following year. In our darkest hours of defeat had been revealed the undying genius of our race. What the ugliness of war had clouded it could not utterly destroy. Surely there had remained even to the end an element of romance, for what more could a man ask than the companionship of brave, loyal, generous men, his country's chivalry? In our hearts there would always be the memory of the undaunted courage, the strength and gentleness of simple men whom we had known.

In the flickering light of the fire the men with whom I had served passed by. How greatly I had been privileged in my friends, and what havoc the war had wrought in that gallant company which even now I could see in the candlelight of the mess in Frechencourt, and whose laughter I could still hear! Noel Blakeway dead at La Boisselle, W. B. Algeo, Harry Mansel Pleydell, dead at Thiepval, Willie Green dead at Leipzig Redoubt, Ian Clarke dead at Beaumont-Hamel, Robin Kestell Cornish dead at Passchendaele! Name after name rose in my mind of others who had gone from the château mess to die on the Somme or in later battles of the war. The hand of Death had been heavy too on my men. Never again would I find my trusted sergeant-major by my side at the head of my company on the march or in the cold light of dawn when the stand-to-arms passed down the expectant lines. There was something of music in their very names, that music which must have stirred the hearts of thousands at memorial services, and has called forth from a Rugby poet some exquisite lines :

> These were my friends. Ah! stay and tell again
> Those lovely names. The grave voice passes on.
> This lantern searching through the field of dead
> Lights one by one the sleepers and is gone.

Dawn came at last, heralding the new life. I laid aside my memories, and set out across Wimbledon Common to the adventure of peace. That adventure did not at first present all the attractions attributed to it in popular report, and I learned how large an element of truth lay in Othello's great cry: " Farewell, the tranquil mind! farewell, content!" which I had quoted in irony as the train left Arquata Scrivia on my journey home.

To me, as to a multitude of other young men, acclimatisation to the conditions of peace was not easy. Since I had left school more than four years before, I had known the world only under the conditions of war. I had no memory of a man's life as it had been before the war on which I might build up a new life for the future. I found it hard to envisage life on an ordered plan covering a period of years; I do not find it easy to-day. Throughout the war, in common with most of the infantry, I had lived solely for the day. In battle and in the front-line trenches we were too much exhausted to conceive anything more distant than the next relief, when we might get some sleep. When we enjoyed a period out of the line, the next leave in England was the farthest point to which the imagination penetrated. I can remember discussions of the world after the war, carried on in a ribald spirit; but I cannot remember seriously discussing the future on any occasion. On Armistice Day the sense of relief was great, but it was accompanied by feelings of bewilderment. For years one set purpose had dominated our lives; that purpose was now fulfilled, and for the moment there was nothing to take its place. For years our lives had been forfeit. We had watched our generation die, not one by one, but in hundreds, throughout four years. Our sorrows had come, not as single spies, but in battalions. So far as we had chosen, or dared, to reflect on the matter, we had known that the hour must come when, in the parlance of the trenches, " our number was up."

Death had been our companion so long that we felt almost at a loss when he left us, and Life took his place.

Our new companion, however welcome, clearly made demands on us to which we were not used. We had to think ahead—a long way ahead. We had to adjust our sense of values, so as to pay adequate regard to the virtues held in honour by a community at peace, which are not the virtues most needed in time of war. Many who had gained a certain satisfaction from the sense that they were wanted in the hour of the country's need found that they were not wanted in the hour of her prosperity; others who had carried the heavy responsibilities of command discovered that henceforward they were to be denied any responsibility. These discoveries were far from welcome. During the war we had comforted ourselves on many occasions by the thought that things are never quite so bad as they seem. Peace, long deferred, was now to teach us the lesson that they are never quite so good.

Moreover, we had time at last to realise how great had been our losses. Day by day the casualty lists had told their tale, but in the preoccupations of the hour their significance had not always been brought home to us. Returning home, we were to hear the full tale. Rugby was no doubt typical of most of the public schools. The school numbered usually between 550 and 560. The number serving in the war was over 3,000, and of these 675 are dead. My own generation probably suffered most. Of the 56 men in my house when I entered it in 1910 no less than 23 lost their lives. But earlier generations were not exempt. One Rugbeian died of wounds received on the first day of the Somme retreat, March 21, 1918, within a few days of his sixty-ninth birthday. This important detail came to the notice of the War Office some time after his death.

Figures are rarely eloquent, but these figures may serve to tell the tale of the losses of my generation; they may illustrate how empty the world seemed to many of us on our return. Throughout our childhood we had looked forward to the great adventure of life. We had had our dreams; in them we had perhaps envisaged life in terms of " high heart, high speech, high deeds 'mid honouring eyes." But always in those dreams the adventure had been shared with our friends. The great game was unthinkable without the companions of our smaller enterprises. But in its place we were given a greater adventure.

Looking back I sometimes think that the shadow of things to come was not wholly absent from our lives. Was Sir James Barrie thinking of the menace of war when he wrote *Peter Pan*? Did no feeling of apprehension darken the mind of any mother in that audience which first heard " My sons shall die like English gentlemen "; did no foreboding enter into the exultation with which those sons first heard youth's defiance of death—" To die would be an awfully big adventure " ?

The adventure of life paled into insignificance before the greater adventure which had been ours. Life, indeed, could no longer be an adventure in the absence of those friends who might have given zest to it. We were indeed rather weary of adventure, and we were conscious of proving a great disappointment to many earnest people who were anxious to recruit us on our return for a variety of crusades at home.

As 1919 wore on I was surprised, in common with many others who fought in the war, at the hatred and bitterness preached and practised by many who had never borne arms, and I was much distressed by the drifting apart into two opposing camps of those who had fought as comrades in the war. The industrial troubles of late 1919 must have depressed me considerably, as some rough notes written at the time, couched in the language of exaggeration, show :

> Everywhere we watch the triumph of the old *régime* and concurrently the inevitable growth of anarchy. And we who fought for a dream of a new world are weary and impotent. We have lost our leaders. We are but a remnant. Our hearts are in the past.

The notes are headed by two lines of John Masefield :

> And all their passionate hearts are dust,
> And dust the great idea that burned.

My gloomy forebodings proved wrong in the event in this, though not in other countries. That they proved wrong, and that our land has been mercifully free from violence, I attribute in a great measure to the determination of those who fought in the war never to engage in civil strife against their late comrades. The advocates of violent courses, on each side, have been drawn almost exclusively from the ranks of those who took no combatant part in the Great War.

A visitor to the battlefields often finds it hard to trace the lines of his old trenches, in so great a degree has the material havoc of the war been made good. It is surely not too much to hope that the moral havoc has disappeared in no less measure. There are other wounds of war which cannot be healed. Nothing can restore to us the men whom we loved, or give to the England of the future the inspiration of their presence, and the men who would have been their sons. Among the men of my generation there are many who must carry during long years the burden of wounds and ill-health, among the women many who must support the greater burden of frustrate lives. The hurrying feet of the years will break us more surely than other generations on which the yoke of inauspicious stars has not pressed.

Not to us will be vouchsafed the opportunity to form a reasoned judgment on those events in which we took part and to determine their place in the scheme of things. We were too busily engaged. We suffered too much. Only after a hundred years are we beginning to understand the Napoleonic wars. And it may be profitable, in considering the issues of the Great War, to turn to that splendid epic, *The Dynasts*, in which the greatest of contemporary writers, through the medium of the Spirit of the Pities, the Ironic Spirit, and the Spirit of the Years meeting on the field of Waterloo and afterwards in the Overworld, spoke his considered judgment on those wars which devastated Europe a century ago, and in the course of their devastation emancipated the mind of man throughout Western Europe.

The Imperial Guard is broken, and the clocks of the world have struck Napoleon's last empery hour; the Spirit of the Pities asks if this is the last Esdraelon of a moil for mortal man's effacement, and the Spirit Ironic replies:

> Warfare mere,
> Plied by the Managed for the Managers;
> To wit: by frenzied folks who profit nought
> For those who profit all!

But the Spirit Ironic has not the last word. The semi-chorus of the Pities speaks of the

Will awaking " in a genial germing purpose, and for loving-kindness' sake."

And at last all the spirits join in one splendid chorus:

But a stirring thrills the air,
Like to sounds of joyance there,
      That the rages
      Of the ages
Shall be cancelled, and deliverance offered from the darts that were,
Consciousness the Will informing, till It fashion all things fair !

No doubt in those years of poverty and disillusion which succeeded the Napoleonic wars the Spirit Ironic was alone heard, and the theory of the impotent and suffering Managed exploited and driven to death by the Managers was as common and as sincerely believed as it is to-day. It is only now that in the chaos and suffering of those wars we can discern any good emerging, any " genial, germing purpose." Perhaps some day later generations may begin to see our war in a truer perspective, and may discern it as an inevitable step in the tragic process by which consciousness has informed the will of man, by which in time all things will be fashioned fair.

Printed in the United States
139626LV00002B/6/A

9 781847 341112